Economics, Law, and Institutions in Asia Pacific

Series Editor

Makoto Yano, Research Institute of Economy, Trade and Industry (RIETI), Tokyo, Japan

The Asia Pacific region is expected to steadily enhance its economic and political presence in the world during the twenty-first century. At the same time, many serious economic and political issues remain unresolved in the region. To further academic enquiry and enhance readers' understanding about this vibrant region, the present series, Economics, Law, and Institutions in Asia Pacific, aims to present cutting-edge research on the Asia Pacific region and its relationship with the rest of the world. For countries in this region to achieve robust economic growth, it is of foremost importance that they improve the quality of their markets, as history shows that healthy economic growth cannot be achieved without high-quality markets. High-quality markets can be established and maintained only under a well-designed set of rules and laws, without which competition will not flourish. Based on these principles, this series places a special focus on economic, business, legal, and institutional issues geared towards the healthy development of Asia Pacific markets. The series considers book proposals for scientific research, either theoretical or empirical, that is related to the theme of improving market quality and has policy implications for the Asia Pacific region. The types of books that will be considered for publication include research monographs as well as relevant proceedings. The series show-cases work by Asia-Pacific based researchers but also encourages the work of social scientists not limited to the Asia Pacific region. Each proposal and final manuscript is subject to evaluation by the editorial board and experts in the field.

More information about this series at http://www.springer.com/series/13451

Makoto Yano · Chris Dai ·
Kenichi Masuda · Yoshio Kishimoto
Editors

Blockchain and Crypto Currency

Building a High Quality Marketplace for Crypto Data

Springer Open

Editors
Makoto Yano
RIETI
Tokyo, Japan

Chris Dai
Recika Co., Ltd
Tokyo, Japan

Kenichi Masuda
Anderson Mori & Tomotsune
Tokyo, Japan

Yoshio Kishimoto
Ministry of Economy, Trade and Industry
Tokyo, Japan

ISSN 2199-8620 ISSN 2199-8639 (electronic)
Economics, Law, and Institutions in Asia Pacific
ISBN 978-981-15-3375-4 ISBN 978-981-15-3376-1 (eBook)
https://doi.org/10.1007/978-981-15-3376-1

This Springer imprint is published by the registered company Springer Nature Singapore Pte Ltd.
The registered company address is: 152 Beach Road, #21-01/04 Gateway East, Singapore 189721, Singapore

Preface

Investment in virtual currency over the past few years appears to have somewhat subsided recently. However, this does not imply that blockchain technology, which underlies virtual currencies, has become less useful. To the contrary, a new generation of blockchains, and their applications, are being actively created and deployed today. The primary purpose of this book is to explore the possibilities of those new blockchains and their applications, to explain the current state of blockchain technologies, and their future use for a wide range of scholars and graduate students beyond their respective fields.

Nowadays, a body of information and communication technology (ICT) and its supporting social system are often perceived as an ecosystem, or, more precisely, a cyber ecosystem. With this term, many people recognize the importance of an ecosystem in which technology and people can coexist in harmony. In this book, we study the design of such a system supported by blockchain technology.

This book investigates the role that the new generation of blockchains may play in the coming data-driven society. It is expected that data will become the third major production factor next to labor and capital in the Internet era. Blockchain technology opens a new way of owning, sharing, and using data.

A blockchain is often defined as a decentralized ledger. "Ledger" is an old term that refers to a "book of a permanent record". A blockchain is a ledger created in a decentralized manner. In this process, many independent entities contribute to creating a book of permanent data that is absolutely accurate and unfalsifiable.

Records that are absolutely accurate and unfalsifiable are valuable. A county recorder's office keeps the vital records that relate to ownership in real estate (land) and to debts or liens upon it. Without these records, it would be practically impossible to trade land and/or to lend and borrow money with land as security. These records are economically valuable because everyone trusts that they are absolutely accurate and unfalsifiable. This trust brings value to the record.

Blockchains have shown that such trusted records can be stored on the Internet in a decentralized manner. The decentralization of the recording process, which has traditionally been centralized and stewarded by the government, is expected to significantly economize transaction costs (or the cost of creating and maintaining a ledger). That is one reason why blockchain technology has been accepted enthusiastically by many.

By making a ledger of data, a blockchain makes it possible to designate the owner of each piece of data, to trade data pieces, and to market them. This book examines the formation of markets for various types of data from the theory of market quality proposed and developed by Yano (for references, see Chap. 4).

Blockchain technology can create a ledger for any type of record. The original Bitcoin blockchain records the transfers of funds between different accounts, thereby providing the same function as deposit currencies that banks offer. If blockchain technology economizes transaction costs significantly, the current monetary system based on central banknotes and deposit currencies may be replaced by a blockchain. Chapter 4 provides an economic analysis of such a possibility, whereas Chap. 5 explains the current state of virtual currency transactions.

Ethereum is a blockchain that is similar to operating systems for PCs and tablets. Like an operating system, it can let independent application programs, called smart contracts, be recorded and executed. On Ethereum, users can execute smart contracts, and results of execution are also recorded securely on Ethereum. This makes it possible for users to develop their own businesses based on smart contract programs and to raise funds for business projects. The possibilities of those businesses and the design of laws and regulations for fundraising for smart-contract-based businesses are discussed in Chaps. 6–8.

Blockchains are expected to give data itself a status of a new production factor. Currently, people hold a great expectation on bigdata created through the Internet of Things (IoT). If all data are shared in various production processes, analyzed by artificial intelligence (AI), and if the results of data analysis are fed back to production processes, productivity may improve drastically. However, data sharing does not progress easily because of the fear of information leakage. Moreover, there is growing concern over data monopoly and data misuse; much of the data created through the Internet is accumulating in the hands of large Internet companies. By bringing the ownership of data into the hands of data producers, blockchains are expected to reduce the possibility of information leakage, enhance the sharing and use of IoT data, and prevent data monopoly and misuse. For this purpose, the current blockchain technology is not sufficiently advanced, and new technology is being developed. Chapters 2 and 3 cover the economic issues on data ownership and the current state of blockchain technology for IoT data.

In the ICT industry, the economic process through which a set of ICT technologies is born and accepted by users has been referred to as an ecosystem. “Ecosystem” is a widely used term in biology, and describes a natural environment in which various organisms live their own lives. There is a harmonious environment consisting of land, rivers, and forests upon which the sun shines and living things are born, grow, reproduce, and undergo evolutionary changes. It is thought that such an environment (i.e., ecosystem) is essential for healthy development of computer technology.

There is a rich cyberspace on the Internet in which many high-speed servers are connected through optical cables. Many computer engineers develop new software programs. Many people use and evaluate these programs, and only the most useful programs are selected. There are also people who evaluate these processes and invest in promising technologies and software applications. Through these processes, existing technologies are improved, and new technologies are born, leading to the next generation of technology. Such has been the harmonized environment in which the ICT industry has developed.

To support this process of technological progress, we need an ecosystem that harmonizes technology, people, and society as a whole. To that end, not only computer scientists and engineers but also entrepreneurs and business people who create and operate new businesses are indispensable. Experts who understand money and finance are also essential. Even more important are the users of services that the engineers and business people produce. All these people are organically linked, sharing information and contributing to building the ICT infrastructure. To build such infrastructure, the process also requires the involvement of legal and economic experts and policymakers who understand the workings of markets and can facilitate the formation of high-quality markets. A cyber ecosystem refers to this whole picture. For the blockchain industry to develop further, it is necessary to build a healthy cyber ecosystem, the design of which is addressed in this study.

This book is expected to contribute to the creation of such an ecosystem encompassing both academia and business. After many intensive discussion sessions, a group of various experts in computer science/engineering, economics, law, policy, and business have assembled this book. While based on the final report of the study group "Blockchain and Society 5.0—The Creation of a New Marketplace based on Distributed Consensus" at the Research Institute of Economy, Trade, and Industry (RIETI), for which Yano serves as the president, the book is extensively rewritten so that it will appeal to scholars from different fields and graduate students interested in interdisciplinary issues on blockchain and related social and technological issues. Of course, the views expressed in this book are those of the authors, not those of the RIETI.

In organizing the study group and putting together this book, we have received extensive support from members of the RIETI, for which we are deeply indebted. In particular, we are grateful to Chairman Atsushi Nakajima of the RIETI for initiating the study group and for the warm and constant encouragement and to Mr. Masataka Saburi, Ms. Kiriko Tanimoto, and Mr. Takehiro Watanabe of the International Division for the promotion and dissemination of our research. Finally, we are deeply indebted to the president's secretary, Ms. Kyoko Nakamura, for supporting the study group and for checking manuscripts at various stages, which has been a great help while assembling this book.

In preparing this book, we have received very kind help from Springer staff. We are particularly grateful to Ms. Juno Kawakami for her constant encouragement, patience, and support to our project and Mr. Austin Schultz for excellent copy editing.

Recently, blockchain currencies and businesses have been targeted by rather wild speculative activities. Blockchain currencies have been used extensively for money laundering and illegal drug trafficking. Because these activities have given the blockchain industry an image of risky business, social perceptions of blockchain are rather negative. However, if better technology is developed and a healthy market infrastructure can be created to support the blockchain market, the industry will have a bright future. It is our hope that this book will contribute to the creation of a cyber ecosystem in which the blockchain industry will grow in a healthy and prosperous manner.

Tokyo, Japan
January 2020

Makoto Yano
Chris Dai
Kenichi Masuda
Yoshio Kishimoto

The original version of this book was revised: Incorrect Book title and coeditors' affiliations has been updated. The correction to this book can be found at https://doi.org/10.1007/978-981-15-3376-1_9

Contents

Editors and Contributors

About the Editors

Makoto Yano is Chairman of the Research Institute of Economy, Trade and Industry (RIETI); he is also a specially appointed professor at Kyoto University, Jochi University, and Chubu University. He is an internationally known researcher who has made a number of substantial contributions in international trade, market theory, and especially on economic dynamics. His contributions in economic dynamics, for example, are represented by articles in *Econometrica* in 1995 and the *Journal of Economic Theory* in 1996, which explained the conditions under which general economic equilibrium shows chaotic behavior. His 1998 *Econometrica* article is recognized as the latest most important work on the characterization of dynamic general equilibrium.

Besides those rather theoretical works, Prof. Yano has also provided influential insights on contemporary real-world phenomena. Those include transfer problems (*American Economic Review*, 1999), voluntary export restraints (*International Economic Review* [IER], 1995), and trade conflicts (IER, 1998), on which there have been a number of follow-up papers.

His recent research on "market quality" addresses various problems in modern economies, including the financial market crisis since 2008 and the recent nuclear accidents in Japan, from the point of view of market quality—a new economic concept that Prof. Yano has developed and is applying to Japanese and international markets. Concerning quality of competition, quality of information, and quality of products, market quality is defined as an index jointly determined by the efficiency of an allocation and the fairness of the prices that are achieved in a market.

Prof. Yano received a B.A. in economics from The University of Tokyo in 1971 and a Ph.D. in economics from The University of Rochester in 1981.

Chris Dai is the CEO and co-founder of Leland Capital, Recika Co., Ltd., and CEO of LongHash Japan. He has a broad range of business management and investment experience. He was formerly the COO/CIO of Yixing SCM (an international logistics provider), a consultant at Accenture, and a co-founder of multiple ventures. Starting in 2013, Mr. Dai was one of the early investors in Bitcoin and Ethereum. To promote the understanding of blockchain's true value, he joined the Research Institute of Economy, Trade and Industry's blockchain research team. He received a B.S. in management science and engineering from Stanford University in 2004.

Kenichi Masuda has been a partner at the law firm of Anderson, Mori & Tomotsune since 1997. He graduated from The University of Tokyo in 1986. After completing work at the Judicial Research and Training Institute, he was admitted to the bar in Japan and joined the law firm in 1988. He graduated from The University of Chicago Law School in 1992 and was admitted to the bar of the State of New York in 1993.

Mr. Masuda has extensive experience in advising foreign clients and is familiar with cross-border issues, in particular, mergers and acquisitions of listed and unlisted businesses, joint ventures, and other cross-border investments, as well as corporate restructuring. The scope of his experience also includes assisting and representing venture companies and establishing venture capital or other private equity funds. He regularly provides legal services on employment and labor union relations (including representation of client companies in court and other dispute-resolution forums), real property transactions, intellectual property issues, and general corporate and commercial matters.

Mr. Masuda currently teaches at The University of Tokyo Law School as a visiting professor.

Yoshio Kishimoto is director general of International Policy for Small and Medium-Sized Enterprises (SMEs), Ministry of Economy, International Trade and Industry. He was vice president of the Research Institute of Economy, International Trade and Industry with Professor Yano.

He has held various positions in METI including head of the Environment and Economy Office, Business Support Division of the SME Agency, and director general of the Kyushu Bureau of METI. He received his M.A. in international affairs from Columbia University in 1992 and a Bachelor of Law degree from The University of Tokyo in 1985.

Contributors

Chris Dai Recika Co., Ltd., Tokyo, Japan;
Leland Capital, Hong Kong, Hong Kong

Yoshio Kishimoto Ministry of Economy, International Trade and Industry, Tokyo, Japan

Kenichi Masuda Anderson Mori & Tomotsune, Tokyo, Japan

William Metcalfe Curvegrid, Tokyo, Japan

Kazumasa Omote University of Tsukuba, Tsukuba, Japan

Steven Pu Taraxa, San Jose, CA, USA

Makoto Yano Research Institute of Economy, Trade and Industry (RIETI), Tokyo, Japan

Chapter 1
Creation of Blockchain and a New Ecosystem

Makoto Yano, Chris Dai, Kenichi Masuda and Yoshio Kishimoto

The Japanese Ministry of Economy, Trade, and Industry regards the process of incorporating new information technology, such as artificial intelligence (AI), Internet of Things (IoT), and big data analysis into society as the Fourth Industrial Revolution. This view is reflected in the Fifth Science and Technology Basic Plan. The plan advocates Society 5.0, in which cyber space and physical space are integrated to support an affluent and human-friendly society. Computer scientists regard the interconnection of industry and society through information technologies, with people creating and using such technologies, as a single ecosystem. They have actively participated in the design and discussion of such an integrated ecosystem. Blockchain is considered to be at the core of such a cyber ecosystem.

Terms like the Fourth Industrial Revolution, Society 5.0, and cyber ecosystems seem colorful and might appear rather farfetched. However, when placed in the context of the current states of the economy and technological development, one

The original version of this chapter is written as a part of our final report to the study group "Blockchain and Society 5.0—The Creation of a New Marketplace based on Distributed Consensus" at the Research Institute of Economy, Trade, and Industry (RIETI). The authors are grateful to all the participant in the study group; the first author gratefully acknowledges the financial support of a Grant-in-Aid for Scientific Research (A) (#16H02015) from the Japan Society for the Promotion of Science.

M. Yano (✉)
Research Institute of Economy, Trade and Industry (RIETI), Tokyo, Japan
e-mail: yano-makoto@rieti.go.jp

C. Dai
Recika Co., Ltd, Tokyo, Japan
e-mail: chris@recika.jp

K. Masuda
Anderson Mori & Tomotsune, Tokyo, Japan

Y. Kishimoto
Ministry of Economy, Trade and Industry, Tokyo, Japan

M. Yano et al. (eds.), *Blockchain and Crypto Currency*,
Economics, Law, and Institutions in Asia Pacific,
https://doi.org/10.1007/978-981-15-3376-1_1

realizes that the new concepts are rather persuasive. This is because the technological innovation that is about to start is very unique in the long history of technological advancement since the First Industrial Revolution.

Today, we are witnessing the introduction of a new type of productive resource into our economy—data. Data is a new productive resource that had no economic value in the past. Until a few years ago, there was no way to gather large volumes of data that could capture daily life accurately, nor were there any computing technologies that made it possible to analyze an extremely large volume of data to explain complicated human interactions on both production and consumption sides of an economy. This has changed all of a sudden. Many productive resources, such as coal and oil, suddenly became valuable during past industrial revolutions. However, they merely replaced already existing resources. Coal replaced firewood and charcoal; oil replaced coal. Data, in contrast, does not replace any existing resources but is born as a completely new type of productive resource.

In short, industrial revolution in the past meant destroying existing resources and replacing them with new resources. Sitting in the middle of the Fourth Industrial Revolution, in contrast, data does not replace any existing resources.

From an economic viewpoint, this difference between past industrial revolutions and the Fourth Industrial Revolution is large. Previously, the ownership of oil was assigned to the owner of the land containing the oil, just as the ownership of coal was assigned before oil was utilized as a major energy source. In the case of data, we have not established a clear agreement on who owns the data. As Nobel laureate Ronald Coase (1910–2013) pointed out, the assignment of proper ownership rights is a prerequisite for the formation of a market.

In these circumstances, blockchain technology opens important avenues to make efficient and fair use of data. In a broader sense, this technology is also referred to as a "decentralized ledger," which can involve a large number of unspecified people to contribute to the effective and fair use of data in a decentralized manner.

In summary, blockchain is expected to play an important role in connecting information technology and technologies such as AI, IoT, and big data with our lives. From this point of view, this book investigates the roles that blockchain plays in a virtual ecosystem from various angles, in particular, from the following three viewpoints: (1) data ownership, (2) data transactions, and (3) data industry.

1 Data: A New Productive Resource

If you are a smart phone user, it must be impossible to think of a day without access to the Internet. A mechanism to assign unique numbers to various things and integrate them into the Internet is called the Internet of Things (IoT). Smartphones are all recognized as IoT terminals, identified by their unique identifiers called telephone numbers, and, now, play a central role in data storage on the Internet.

With the exception of the phone function, almost all the information acquired through smartphones is provided through the Internet. At the same time, we have become an important source of information. Buying goods through Amazon is like offering part of your household account book. When using Facebook and the "like" function is used, some sort of preference is expressed toward society. Sending emails also implies providing information to society.

It is not only humans that can be connected with cyber space through IoT. Computer sensors can be placed on livestock in pasture to keep track of their health and nutritional needs. If sensors are attached to trees and every square meter of farmland, the growth conditions of trees and vegetables in every square meter of the field can be monitored. In this way, a new ecosystem of human beings and living things, with information technology as infrastructure, can be created. Sensors on a car can keep track of driving habits, which is useful to enhance driving safety. Similarly, sensors in a hospital room can monitor and report the state of each patient and give useful information to carers. In this way, we can create a new ecosystem based on information and communication technology.

In the ecosystem, all information is digitized and recorded as numbers. This is why the information exchanged in IoT is called data. With modern computer technology, huge volumes of data can be collected and scientifically analyzed in detail to gain insights into various phenomena much deeper and clearer than possible only 10 years ago. Results from data analysis have started to profoundly influence our society.

This has transformed data into a new type of productive resource, by which we can manage production processes in a much more precise manner. With data on people's medical histories, doctors will be able to diagnose a patient's illness much more accurately and give better or more appropriate treatments. With data on car driving, insurance companies will evaluate driving risks much more accurately, thus allowing them to reduce insurance fees where appropriate. With data on purchases in stores, both manufacturers and retailers have increased ability to market attractive products to customers. All these possibilities are brought about by the data-gathering capability of the Internet and the data-processing capabilities of modern computers.

2 Blockchain Technology

Blockchain may still be a new term for many readers. It is, therefore, appropriate to start with a discussion on the definition of blockchain.

A ledger is a book of permanent record. The record must be correct and tamper-free. A blockchain is a ledger that is put together on the Internet in a decentralized manner by an indefinite number of contributors.

Blockchain is a chain of files containing whatever needs to be permanently recorded. A basic blockchain connects files to form a simple string of chain. A more sophisticated blockchain connects files to form a net-like structure.

2.1 Blockchain and Data Ownership

A database is like an address book in which many data elements are stored systematically and organized for easy use. Blockchain is a new technology that allows us to record data and sources and recipients of data exchanged on the Internet, thereby creating an accurate, permanent, and very inexpensive database.

The first application of blockchain technology was the virtual currency called Bitcoin. Functionally, a virtual currency is much the same as a deposit currency that is based on bank accounts. Each bank account records debits to and credits from other accounts, which the bank keeps to be absolutely accurate and tamper-free. Because the record shows who owes how much to whom, and because people trust that the records are absolutely reliable, it can be used to transfer money through wire transfers; debit cards are a major means of payment nowadays. A virtual currency is a similar collection of accounts (called wallets) that record debits and credits. The difference is that the virtual currency accounts are on the Internet. Blockchain technology has made it possible to keep this record absolutely reliable by using algorithm without relying on a central authority like a bank.

Blockchain accounts record digital data, which plays the role of money because people trust that they are accurate and tamper-free. As this shows, blockchain can assign the ownership of each data piece to an account holder. This is the innovation that blockchain technology has brought to society.

2.2 Distributed Computing

Distributed computing is a revolutionary innovation in computer networks, which allows many terminal computers to perform complicated tasks independently (Holohan and Garg 2005). One good example is a category of games called "massively multiplayer online games" in which many different players participate and try to achieve their respective goals, which may vary from car racing to shooting to role playing. Blockchain technology is built on this idea of distributed computing and adds decentralization to enable individual participants to maintain a secure record of transactions, ownerships, and promises.

The initial design of a computer network, which connects many computers to share resources, is centrally managed. In building a centralized network, a network administrator is chosen, a large server computer is set up, a network connecting many computers is designed, and software is installed on the server and made available for network users. The administrator centrally manages users' network connections, and only users with connection permission can use the network. The networks of companies and universities are designed in this way, and the same is true for online banking systems that connect automatic teller machines (ATMs). In a centrally managed network, the terminal computers perform very minimal tasks. For example, a bank ATM terminal recognizes the account number and the password, and then performs simple tasks such as deposits and withdrawals.

As a network becomes larger, it becomes more and more difficult to maintain a centralized network. The load on the central server increases, and the cost of managing the server becomes very large. Central servers can also become very attractive targets for malicious attacks, and once these servers are compromised, the entire system can be destroyed.

A distributed network is built by connecting various independent servers and computers. Various tasks are distributed to different servers, and altogether a single goal can be achieved. A large volume of tasks are assigned to terminal computers. As long as basic rules for connecting to the network are set and those rules are followed, any server and any computer can join the network.

Such rules are called protocols. In the most immediate example, the email address is separated by the at-mark, @; the part after the "at mark" is an address indicating a particular computer group; the part before is an individual in that group. This rule is a very small part of the large Internet protocol.

A distributed network makes it possible to utilize a large portion of the computing power of the computers in a network. The various computers connected to the network perform large tasks by computing independently while coordinating tasks through exchange of data. Having a large number of computers work independently can achieve great goals at very low cost.

2.3 *Blockchain: Decentralized Ledger*

Distributed computing has evolved as a computer network construction method. Blockchain is a technology that builds a ledger based on distributed computing in a decentralized manner. This might sound simple, but, in reality, it is not. To create a decentralized ledger, it is necessary to devise a totally new algorithm, and such work led to the creation of Bitcoin.

To create and maintain a secure decentralized ledger, it is not enough to use a security program; such security measures can be easily breached by experienced hackers. Even if many independent computers maintain ledger together with good intentions, they are still vulnerable to attacks by computers with malicious intentions. This is especially so if such a ledger maintains records that function as money or virtual currency, where absolute accuracy and permanence are required.

This problem was overcome by the first blockchain, known as Bitcoin. In most blockchain, the database is shared by a large number of servers. Each server stores the entire blockchain record and carries out similar jobs in parallel. These servers are called full nodes of a blockchain. A new server that wants to join a blockchain network is free to copy the blockchain record and download the necessary software to store the records. Once in a while, the records on participating servers are synchronized so that only one record is produced. With more nodes, the number of copies of the blockchain's ledger throughout the world increases, which makes it extremely difficult for malicious computers to attack the blockchain.

The decentralized ledger database is linked with user accounts called wallets. A wallet is a record of a particular user's transactions, which is kept on the user's terminal computer. Once a transaction between two accounts is agreed upon, the account owners apply to the blockchain to record the transaction. In most of the existing blockchains, recorders of transactions are different from users who use a blockchain as a currency. In some blockchains, users of a blockchain record their transactions by themselves.

2.4 Mining

The Bitcoin blockchain uses "mining" to maintain the accuracy and reliability of transaction records.[1] Mining in the context of blockchain technology is to present a computer-generated crypto puzzle to individuals (computers), to give a prize (in Bitcoin) to the individual who solves the puzzle first, and to let the individual record the transaction. In competing for the prize, many people (computers) engage in solving the crypto puzzle to create transaction records. With only one individual out of many competitors receiving the prize, this process is similar to mining; and individuals engaging in solving puzzles are called miners.

As soon as a mining computer solves the existing puzzle, a new file (block) is created and attached to the existing chain of blocks. The new block creates a new puzzle to be solved. At the same time, the solution is announced to the network of mining computers. Mining computers check if that solution is correct. If the solution is in fact correct, mining computers start working on solving the new puzzle created by the block that they have just validated.

In this entire process, it is important that there is no single individual who is in charge of checking the validity and uniqueness of records on blockchain. Instead, many independent individuals check the validity of records, which produces a unique record (ledger). This process is completely decentralized.

For Bitcoin blockchain, on one hand, simple records of several transactions are put together and recorded as a new block. On the other hand, for Ethereum blockchain, user-executable computer programs and resulting transactions of executing the programs can be written into a new block by a mining node.

A problem with blockchains is that mining consumes computer resources not directly related to records. Many miners work on solving the puzzle posed by the blockchain. Because this puzzle can be solved by a sequence of computations, anyone can find an answer so long as he/she is prepared to spend enough computing resources.

As a result, if there are 1,000 miners, the computational resources used by 999 miners (i.e., electricity to run computations) will be wasted. As the value of virtual currency soars, the number of miners has increased dramatically, and it is said that

---

[1] For the technical side of mining, see Omote and Yano.

about 10,000 miners are active around the world. Given that the average time required to solve the puzzle is 10 min, it is possible that a huge amount of electricity is being wasted. To maintain the accuracy of the blockchain, a certain number of miners must be involved. Whether electricity is wasted is related to the number of miners required to maintain accuracy.

2.5 Advancement of Blockchain Technology

The Bitcoin blockchain proved that a secure ledger can be created in a decentralized manner without using a trusted authority who is specialized in managing a ledger. Since then, different types of blockchains have been created.

A blockchain called IOTA creates a blockchain model that is not based on mining, hence does not consume a large amount of electricity. The IOTA blockchain is not a linear chain of files as used by the Bitcoin blockchain. Instead, it has a very complicated network structure, which itself is impossible to replicate. This structure is called a directed acyclic graph (DAG). Each transaction file (block) is given two arms, each of which randomly grabs another file (directed from grabbing to grabbed files). As the number of files becomes larger, the number of arms increases by the power of 2, which soon becomes an extremely complicated structure. In this structure, a sequence of files is created in which a particular file grabs another file, which will grab the next, and so on. It has been shown that if such a sequence never contains a circle (acyclic), the structure can serve as a blockchain, which can dispense with the requirement for mining.

A few years after Bitcoin was introduced, a new blockchain called Ethereum was developed. It was able to execute any program and to create execution records, as well as record transactions.

Not only does Ethereum provide its own virtual currency, called Ether, it also works in conjunction with Ether to provide a "platform" for loading and executing programs. These programs are called smart contracts, which can program the execution of a promise between users with various contingencies.

Once a business can be run on a blockchain, business developers seek funding to further develop the business or for future businesses. Such funding is also carried out over the Internet in a manner similar to crowd funding. This method of funding is called ICO (initial coin offering), and it sells and collects funds for business vouchers called tokens.

3 Building a People-Friendly Ecosystem

Information technologies such as AI, IoT, and big data are expected to contribute greatly to the realization of a new human-friendly ecosystem. However, it is a mistake to think that such an ecosystem will be built if technological innovation is realized.

The modern economy faces major problems of data monopoly and data abuse. Society 5.0 can be formed only after overcoming these problems.

3.1 Society 5.0

The blueprint of Society 5.0 as advocated by the Japanese government is based on the following loop: collection of data from every part of society by IoT, creation of big data, data analysis by AI, and injection of results of data analysis back to society.

The government states, "In the information society (Society 4.0), cross-sectional sharing of knowledge and information was not enough, and cooperation was difficult."[2] It continues, "Social reform (innovation) in Society 5.0 will achieve a forward-looking society that breaks down the existing sense of stagnation, a society whose members have mutual respect for each other, transcending the generations, and a society in which each and every person can lead an active and enjoyable life."

The government argues, "Society 5.0 achieves a high degree of convergence between cyberspace (virtual space) and physical space (real space)…In the past information society, the common practice was to collect information via the network and have it analyzed by humans. In Society 5.0, however, people, things, and systems are all connected in cyberspace and optimal results obtained by AI exceeding the capabilities of humans are fed back to physical space. This process brings new value to industry and society in ways not previously possible." However, it is a mistake to assume that so long as technological innovation progresses, the image of Society 5.0 will naturally be realized without any effort.

3.2 Industrial Revolution and Market Quality

Since the First Industrial Revolution, industrialization has brought about the concentration of resources in specific industries and companies. Yano (2009) views this process as a dynamical system of technology and market quality.[3] According to Yano, massive technological progress lowers market quality. This brings about various social problems; essentially, the concentration of resources causes fundamental changes in lifestyle and social structure. Once market quality falls to a certain level, however, demand will increase because of accumulated knowledge and experience, which will stimulate new innovation (Yano and Furukawa 2019).

The First Industrial Revolution (1760s to the 1840s) began with the invention of steam engines in England. The textile industry underwent major technological

[2]https://www8.cao.go.jp/cstp/english/society5_0/index.html.

[3]For a further analysis on market quality, see Yano (2019).

innovation, many workers were hired, capital was invested, and production expanded. Instead of engaging in in-house production activities, people were hired in large factories. Capital was accumulated by companies rather than by individuals. This resulted in the exploitation of workers, which Karl Marx (1818–1883) criticized harshly (Marx 1867). The Second Industrial Revolution came with steel production, railways, large-scale iron and steel production, electricity, telegraphs and telephones, and machinery. Major companies became enormous, and were perceived as a menace to society (Hilferding 1910).

3.3 *Data Monopoly and Data Abuse*

Yano's theory applies to the recent progress brought about by the technological revolution in information and communication technology (ICT revolution). One of the most successful groups of companies after the turn of the century is GAFA, which represents the initials of Google, Amazon, Facebook, and Apple. These companies were very successful during the ICT revolution, and, in doing so, have collected large volumes of data.

This concentration of resources realized economies of scale and production efficiency. Nevertheless, many people are worried about data concentration on GAFA (Radingsky 2015).

This worry is not imaginary but real, as shown by the recent abuse of data collection by Cambridge Analytica. Cambridge Analytica is alleged to have collected the personal data of 230 million Americans through Facebook accounts and used it to influence voters in favor of Donald Trump in the 2016 US presidential election (Cadwalladr 2018).The original method of data collection, which was developed by two psychologists, was to offer an Internet-based psychological test for anyone interested, and, at the end of the test seek permission to access the respondent's Facebook profile. According to Cadwalladr (2018), 40% of the respondents gave permission. By using the data, the psychologists were able to measure personality traits and to correlate scores against Facebook "likes" for millions of people. This method was adopted by Cambridge Analytica, which obtained personal data and then devised methods to influence important votes such as the US presidential election and the Brexit referendum.

This is a clear warning that data can be badly abused by monopolizing it. Unless these problems are resolved, the integration of cyber and physical spaces may end up with a rather dark society that is far from the image presented by the Society 5.0 initiative. Avoiding the emergence of such a dark society is a pressing issue that we now face (Economist 2018).

3.4 Small to Medium-Sized Enterprises

Many people say that in the digital economy, data is a production factor equivalent to oil. Data needs to be shared and distributed throughout society if it is to be used effectively in the digital age. So far, however, data has accumulated in the hands of large companies trying to establish competitive advantage. As a result, data is just stored, and it is becoming more difficult for small and medium-sized companies to use data for innovation.

For small to medium-sized enterprises, an even bigger problem is that they do not have good access to human resources specialized in handling data. This has created an egg-or-chicken paradox. To break such a vicious cycle, we require a good ecosystem that allows everyone to own and trade data and utilize the results of data analysis.

To resolve these problems, blockchain technology is ideal. It can be expected to release data to every productive sector, thereby enhancing the productivity of the economy as a whole.

4 Organization of This Book

As discussed above, the integration of cyber space and physical space will not automatically lead to the creation of a human-friendly society unless a sound interface is created between such a society and data as a new economic resource. The main purpose of this book is to investigate the role of blockchains as such an interface. In particular, we focus on the roles of blockchains from three viewpoints: (1) data ownership, (2) data transactions, and (3) the data industry.

4.1 Data Ownership

Many people think that as the IoT becomes more important in the production process, data will become an increasingly important production factor. To make good use of these new resources, it is necessary to start with setting ownership. In Chapter 2, Steven Pu and Makoto Yano cover this issue in the context of market quality theory.

As pointed out by Ronald Coase, a resource cannot be put on a market unless proper ownership is assigned to the resource. Many people say that data in a coming digital economy is a production factor equivalent to oil for the existing economy.

To whom should ownership be assigned for such an important production factor? It is our view that the ownership of data should belong to the originator of data so as to avoid inefficient and unfair use of data, which may result from monopoly and abuse of data.

Currently, most data that we produce is collected and accumulated by large Internet data companies, as presented by GAFA. Such data is kept in a black box, and there is no way for ordinary people to know how it is used. For the oil industry, on the one hand, everyone has a relatively clear understanding on the supply chain from producers to consumers. In the case of data, on the other hand, how it is used is kept under a veil.

For data to play an equally important role as oil in digital society, it must be shared and used by many people. Nevertheless, an increasing number of large companies are monopolizing data to establish a competitive advantage. Being stored in large companies, it is becoming increasingly difficult for small and medium-sized companies to use data for innovation. On the other hand, for large companies, there is no strong incentive to use data; it is adequate to hold the information to deter challenges from competitors. How can we improve this situation?

The first step is to return ownership of the data to the individual who produces it. Blockchains make it possible to record data ownership at a low cost. Once the ownership of data is decided, data can be traded. To assign proper ownership of IoT data and put it on a market, it is necessary to develop a new blockchain technology. In Chapter 3, Steven Pu explains the development of this technology.

4.2 Data as Money

As an increasing number of people accept Bitcoin and other virtual currencies, a number of associated problems have arisen, such as money laundering, transactions of illegal drugs, and speculative activities. If these problems are not resolved, virtual currencies may not circulate widely. At the same time, however, blockchain technology itself has shown that data can be used as money. It can create a reliable record (ledger) of transactions in a decentralized manner without a central administrator. In Chapter 4, Makoto Yano investigates the possibility that such a decentralized ledger currency can take over the conventional deposit currency and paper money, once the existing problems are overcome.

4.3 Data Industry

As noted above, Ethereum is a technology that makes it possible to run any program and to record the results on blockchain. This opens up an infinitely large possibility for blockchain business.

The market in which data is traded on blockchain is often called a marketplace. In a marketplace, anything can be traded from candy to golf club memberships. These transactions are made by software applications called decentralized applications (DApps). In Chapter 5, William Metcalfe explains the role of smart contracts in Ethereum and the current state of DApp technology and their applications.

In a blockchain marketplace, all transaction records are made public. In exchanges for virtual currencies, in contrast, they are not made public; in this respect, they are similar to marketplaces such as Amazon. For this reason, a virtual currency exchange can be called a centralized marketplace. Centralized marketplaces present themselves as a single point of failure, and, therefore, are prone to malicious attacks. Moreover, they lack transparency such that the actions of the organizer of a centralized market cannot be monitored by outsiders.

A bottleneck of the current virtual currency system is the time needed to carry out transactions. To overcome this problem and to provide more convenient transactions, an exchange market for virtual currency has been developed. However, the existing virtual currency exchanges are centrally controlled by exchange organizers. As a result, they are prone to malicious attacks, and in fact, a number of hacking incidents on exchange has been reported.[4]

The decentralized exchange (DEX) is a new DApp that has been developed to cope with this weak points of centralized marketplaces. DEX allows a seller and a buyer of crypto assets to make a direct exchange in a decentralized manner on blockchain. Data (crypto assets and transaction records) is held in a decentralized manner so that DEX does not present itself as a single point of failure to attackers. Furthermore, because the system is open to the public, transactions can be made in a much more transparent fashion. It is offered in exchange for investments in DApp development. In Chapter 6, Chris Dai explains DApps and DEX and explains the current state of token business.

A token is a device to raise funds for developing blockchains and blockchain applications (DApps). A token can be thought of as a ticket for using the services that a DApp promises to offer. It is offered in exchange for investments in DApp development.

The introduction of fundraising by token issuance may be a result of the decentralized nature of blockchain technologies. Because of decentralization, the start-up process of blockchain businesses is significantly different from that of conventional businesses. In the current state of society, in which blockchains are not yet established, it may be desirable to treat start-up blockchain businesses like venture investments. However, once the technology is established, a new decentralized financial system will become necessary. From these perspectives, in Chapter 7, we consider the desirable designs for a decentralized financial system for both short-term and long-term scenarios.

The main message of this study is that it is important to build an ecosystem in which the new technology (blockchain), laws and institutions, including data ownership,

[4]For a list of hacking incidences, see SELFKEY (2019), https://selfkey.org/list-of-cryptocurrency-exchange-hacks/,downloaded.

and markets for digital assets are harmonized. Market quality theory suggests that the ownership of big data collected through the Internet should be assigned in such a way to support high-quality digital data markets. See Chapters 2 and 7 for a discussion on desirable designs of the decentralized financial system from these perspectives.

In Chapter 8, Kazumasa Omote and Makoto Yano discuss the blockchain technology on which Bitcoin is based.

Appendix

As shown in Fig. 1, modern networks can be divided into three types: centralized, distributed, and decentralized. The Internet is a revolutionary technology that has transformed centralized networks into distributed and more decentralized networks. Blockchain is a technology that has made it possible to build a completely decentralized network on the Internet. However, the Internet is far less decentralized than a blockchain, meaning that a government can block Internet access for computers, as has been done in China. The network system of a blockchain, in contrast, cannot be directly interfered with by a government.

When creating a network there are three topologies to choose from: centralized, distributed, and decentralized. As mentioned above, a computer connected on a network is called a node. In a centralized network, a computer called a central node owns and manages the entire network. The central node is a single point of contact for information sharing, controlling access to all calculations and data, and storing data.

The biggest problem with centralized networks is that the central node becomes a single point of failure. In other words, if the central node is broken, the entire network will crash. Attackers can break the entire network by bringing down the central node. Also, because the network workload is concentrated on the central node, the larger the network, the greater the load on the central node.

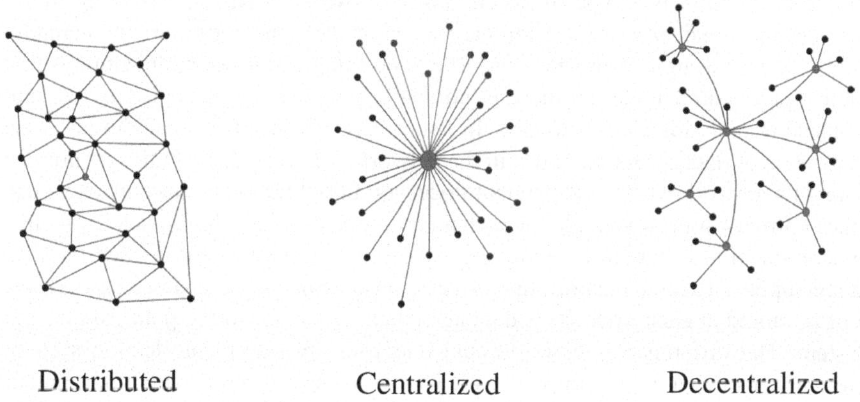

Fig. 1 Different types of networks

A distributed network is based on the concept of distributed computing. The Internet is a representative example. In a distributed network such as the Internet, each participating node performs computation and data storage independently but *appears to its users as a coherent system.* This eliminates the problem of single point of failure that can occur in centralized networks. Because nodes are independent, even if a particular node fails, information can be accessed from other nodes.

In a distributed network such as the Internet, there is no single central node. However, many nodes are similar to the central node of a centralized network and are located to perform management tasks. Such management nodes control the distribution of workload on the network and authenticate network participants. As a result, the work of the network is optimally distributed among the nodes and calculation processing is performed. Some distributed networks also have peer-to-peer networks, with only completely identical nodes without a central node. However, in this case, network-wide sharing of the same data is very difficult.

If a distributed open network is chosen to maintain a universal ledger instead of a centralized network, we need to eliminate the participation of malicious nodes. In this case, it is necessary to develop a special protocol to protect data and computations from spamming and incorrect data sent from malicious nodes. Blockchain technology makes this possible by utilizing an algorithm that protects data and computations from malicious nodes by majority vote of participating nodes. A calculation procedure (algorithm) based on blockchain technology is called a decentralized consensus formation algorithm or simply a "consensus algorithm." Such a network is called a decentralized and distributed network in the sense that it fully addresses malicious attacks based on majority agreements, and is distinguished from distributed networks that do not synchronize data across the network.

Consensus Among Blockchain Nodes

Public blockchain is a type of decentralized network. Nodes participating in the network independently execute software based on the same algorithm and maintain coordination throughout the network. The good thing about decentralization is that there is no central node, so there is no single point of failure and it is resistant to hacking and single node failure. Instead, there is a need to maintain common awareness of data across all nodes in the network. It is very difficult to synchronize data on a network where independent nodes are unstable (sometimes attackers can take control of some nodes). In blockchain protocol, the algorithm for achieving this synchronization is called the consensus algorithm. Consensus means that the data agreed upon across the network (majority of the nodes) will be reviewed and a copy will be stored at each node. This data agreement is similar to the political election system. The difference is how to count one vote. In a political election system, normally one person can cast one vote. However, there is no concept of "number of people" in the network of nodes (computers).To prevent the same person from voting more than once, the unit of voting must be such that a network of computers can understand and quantify. For consensus algorithms such as proof-of-work (PoW) computational power is the unit of vote. For proof-of-stake (PoS), the unit of vote is the number of tokens you own or "stake." Unlike political elections, blockchain consensus (voting) is run much more frequently and automatically. For example, in the case of Bitcoin, consensus is reached at 10-minute intervals with the creation of a new block.

Sharding

Given that complete blockchain data is recorded on all full nodes as a feature of blockchain, it takes considerable time to synchronize and create new blocks (data) with a consensus algorithm on all nodes. As a result, blockchains like Bitcoin and Ethereum can only record about 7–26 transactions per second for the entire network. This is too slow for many applications. One solution designed to increase blockchain data recording/processing throughput is sharding. Even before the invention of blockchain, sharding was used to speed up database access by dividing the database to several parts and distributing the parts to several separate servers. Applying the same concept to a blockchain, rather than obtaining consensus from all nodes and then adding a new block (synchronization), groups (shard) of nodes can be created and if consensus can be reached within the group of nodes then a new block can be added.

Theoretically, with more shards and more blocks added in parallel, the overall network throughput becomes higher. However, while throughput can be improved, sharding also presents serious challenges. For example, with more shards, the number of nodes in a shard becomes less and they are more vulnerable to attacks. In addition, because it is also possible to process transactions across shards in what is a complicated process, there are concerns about both vulnerability and throughput of transactions.

Scalability and Decentralization

Scalability in blockchain refers to the speed at which blockchain can add transaction records and reach consensus across the network. Decentralization can be thought of as a measure of how independently nodes or computers agree on a set of transactions without central direction and control. As the system becomes more decentralized, it becomes more independent and the records become more tamper resistant from external monitoring and censorship. Technically, there is clear trade-off between the three factors characterizing a blockchain—scalability, safety, and decentralization. However, regardless of the purpose for which the blockchain is used, security is usually not a feature that can be sacrificed. In most situations, what matters is the trade-off between scalability and decentralization. Sharding, described in the previous section, is a technology introduced to improve scalability.

During the early stage of blockchain application development, emphasis was placed on decentralization. As a result, technical performance and usability were sacrificed. For example, in a blockchain Dapp, the user is only given a password for login once and if lost, the user account cannot be recovered, and, as a result, the assets stored in the account will be completely lost. This maybe acceptable for an engineer who values the fact the password is not kept on someone else's server. However, most people are used to an environment where their account can be reissued or reset if the password is lost. To appeal to the general public, Dapps must centralize the password management to a certain degree to allow for unintended user errors.

Token Price: Security or Utility

During early development of the Bitcoin program, a whitepaper and prototype protocol were released and the open-source community worked together to ensure reliability and credibility based on the good intentions of ordinary engineers interested in the program. However, in such collaboration based purely on good faith, it is also difficult to secure enough resources to commercialize a blockchain project. In recent blockchain projects, financing was obtained by ICO (initial coin offering). A typical ICO sells a ticket for a service called a token.

The ICO fundraising method is often abused as a method to evade the securities law. If a token is recognized as a means of investment, it leads to speculative purchasing. As a result, prices can soar and be higher than their actual value. For example, during 2018, when the price of Bitcoin rose, it cost $10 to transfer $100 for Bitcoin. In this case, the Bitcoin transaction fee was higher than that of bank transfer and credit card, and therefore was not suitable to be used for payment.

An even bigger problem is that the token prices of blockchain-based applications fluctuate significantly due to speculation. The price of Bitcoin rose sharply in 2017 and dropped significantly in 2018. For speculators, price fluctuations provide a profit opportunity, but for actual users who pay cash to purchase tokens to use the blockchain-based applications will be dismayed at the price fluctuation.

Those who are trying to create new blockchain applications and provide them to the market are expected to solve these problems by providing stable tokens or virtual currency. For example, it may be useful to consider automatically adjusting the supply of tokens to price fluctuations, or to introduce an institution with a central bank function. Doing so may allow users to find higher value in blockchain application services. In the future, for the blockchain industry to grow, it is essential that the quality of service improves rather than having more speculative opportunities arise.

Traceability and anonymity

As mentioned earlier, originally, in blockchain, the account and the owner of the account were not linked. Movement of funds in each account was publicized, but only the owner knew who owned the account. In other words, the owner of the account was anonymous. By exploiting the anonymity, it is possible to transfer funds while keeping the identity of the account owner secret. This is very difficult to achieve with the banking system. Thus, blockchain appears to be well suited for use in illegal transactions and money laundering. However, anonymity in blockchain is not perfect, and identities may be uncovered if the system is abused extensively.

This fact is well demonstrated by the case of Silk Road, an illegal drug e-commerce site. Silk Road was launched in February 2011 and provided a marketplace for illegal drug trading until it was closed by the FBI in October 2013. This site provided the seller's account and the buyer's account, and seller's account was able to list products; that is, illegal drugs. The buyer was able to place the order anonymously and made payment using Bitcoin. As a result, the seller and buyer were able to trade the goods anonymously. It is estimated that more than 100,000 buyers and thousands of sellers were involved and more than 1 billion USD was traded before the closure.

By the summer of 2013, the FBI had already started an investigation of Silk Road and identified the IP address (the numerical address assigned to each computer server on the Internet) of the Silk Road site. The person who was operating Silk Road was arrested on charges of money laundering, computer hacking, and illegal drug transactions, and was eventually sentenced to life imprisonment.

As this case demonstrates, the high anonymity provided by blockchain is not absolute. Even if dubious Internet activities do not occur on a largescale like Silk Road, graph/data analysis can be applied to identify and trace fraudulent transactions.

In Japan, a registered virtual currency exchange is obligated to confirm the identity of a customer in accordance with the Crime Revenue Transfer Prevention Act. In addition, the virtual currency exchange manages the customer's deposit wallet and can link the account number and the customer's personal identification information. In this way, as the day-to-day blockchain transactions increase, various insights can be identified from the data, which may prevent crimes and identify suspicious transactions that exploit blockchain anonymity. In the future as more people use blockchain for their transactions in both the physical and cyber world, the protection of privacy for on-chain transactions may become a bigger challenge.

References

Cadwalladr C (2018) 'I made Steve Bannon's Psychological Warfare Tool': Meet the data war whistleblower. Guardian, 18 March 2018

Economist (2018) How to tame the tech titans – the dominance of Google, Facebook and Amazon is bad for consumers and competition. The Economist, 18 January 2018

Hilferding R (1910) Financial capital

Holohan A, Garg A (2005) Collaboration online: the example of distributed computing. J Comput-Mediated Commun 10-4, JCMC10415, https://doi.org/10.1111/j.1083-6101.2005.tb00279.x
Marx K (1867) Capital, vol 1
Radingsky K (2015) Data monopolists like Google are threatening the economy. Harvard Business Review, 02 March 2015
SELFKEY (2019) A comprehensive list of cryptocurrency exchange hacks. Downloaded at https://selfkey.org/list-of-cryptocurrency-exchange-hacks/, on 11 Nov. 2019
Yano M (2009) The foundation of market quality economics. Jpn Econ Rev 60–1(1–32):2009
Yano M (2019) Market quality theory and the coase theorem in the presence of transaction costs. RIETI DP19-E-097
Yano M, Furukawa Y (2019) Two-dimensional constrained chaos and time in innovation: an analysis of industrial revolution cycles. RIETI DP19-E-008

Makoto Yano is Chairman of the Research Institute of Economy, Trade and Industry (RIETI); he is also a specially appointed professor at Kyoto University, Jochi University, and Chubu University. He is an internationally known researcher who has made a number of substantial contributions in international trade, market theory, and especially on economic dynamics. His contributions in economic dynamics, for example, are represented by articles in *Econometrica* in 1995 and the *Journal of Economic Theory* in 1996, which explained the conditions under which general economic equilibrium shows chaotic behavior. His 1998 *Econometrica* article is recognized as the latest most important work on the characterization of dynamic general equilibrium.

Besides those rather theoretical works, Prof. Yano has also provided influential insights on contemporary real-world phenomena. Those include transfer problems (*American Economic Review*, 1999), voluntary export restraints (*International Economic Review* [IER], 1995), and trade conflicts (IER, 1998), on which there have been a number of follow-up papers.

His recent research on "market quality" addresses various problems in modern economies, including the financial market crisis since 2008 and the recent nuclear accidents in Japan, from the point of view of market quality—a new economic concept that Prof. Yano has developed and is applying to Japanese and international markets. Concerning quality of competition, quality of information, and quality of products, market quality is defined as an index jointly determined by the efficiency of an allocation and the fairness of the prices that are achieved in a market. Prof. Yano received a B.A. in economics from The University of Tokyo in 1971 and a Ph.D. in economics from The University of Rochester in 1981.

Chris Dai is the CEO and co-founder of Leland Capital, Recika Co., Ltd., and CEO of LongHash Japan. He has a broad range of business management and investment experience. He was formerly the COO/CIO of Yixing SCM (an international logistics provider), a consultant at Accenture, and a co-founder of multiple ventures. Starting in 2013, Mr. Dai was one of the early investors in Bitcoin and Ethereum. To promote the understanding of blockchain's true value, he joined the Research Institute of Economy, Trade and Industry's blockchain research team. He received a B.S. in management science and engineering from Stanford University in 2004.

Kenichi Masuda has been a partner at the law firm of Anderson, Mori & Tomotsune since 1997. He graduated from The University of Tokyo in 1986. After completing work at the Judicial Research and Training Institute, he was admitted to the bar in Japan and joined the law firm in 1988. He graduated from The University of Chicago Law School in 1992 and was admitted to the bar of the State of New York in 1993.

Mr. Masuda has extensive experience in advising foreign clients and is familiar with cross-border issues, in particular, mergers and acquisitions of listed and unlisted businesses, joint ventures, and other cross-border investments, as well as corporate restructuring. The scope of his experience also includes assisting and representing venture companies and establishing venture capital or other private equity funds. He regularly provides legal services on employment and labor union relations (including representation of client companies in court and other dispute-resolution forums), real property transactions, intellectual property issues, and general corporate and commercial matters.

Mr. Masuda currently teaches at The University of Tokyo Law School as a visiting professor.

Yoshio Kishimoto is director general of International Policy for Small and Medium-Sized Enterprises (SMEs), Ministry of Economy, International Trade and Industry. He was vice president of the Research Institute of Economy, International Trade and Industry with Professor Yano.

He has held various positions in METI including head of the Environment and Economy Office, Business Support Division of the SME Agency, and director general of the Kyushu Bureau of METI. He received his M.A. in international affairs from Columbia University in 1992 and a Bachelor of Law degree from The University of Tokyo in 1985.

Chapter 2
Market Quality Approach to IoT Data on Blockchain Big Data

Steven Pu and Makoto Yano

1 Introduction

The Internet of things (IoT) is considered a key driving force of what the Japanese government refers to as Society 5.0, the image of an ideal future society that the Japanese government currently advocates.[1] Society 5.0 is defined as "a human-centered society that balances economic advancement with the resolution of social problems by a system that integrates cyberspace and physical space." According to the government, "In Society 5.0, a huge amount of information from sensors in physical space is accumulated in cyberspace. In cyberspace, this big data is analyzed by artificial intelligence (AI), and the analysis results are fed back to humans in physical space in various forms." The IoT provides a crucial link between cyberspace and physical space.

[1] For details, see "From Industry 4.0 to Society 5.0: the big societal transformation plan of Japan," i-SCOOP (see https://www.i-scoop.eu/industry-4-0-society-5-0/). Also see http://www8.cao.go.jp/cstp/english/society5_0/index.html and https://www.weforum.org/agenda/2018/07/could-japan-become-a-role-model-for-the-fourth-industrial-revolution/.

This is based on our final report to the study group "Blockchain and Society 5.0—The Creation of a New Marketplace based on Distributed Consensus" at the Research Institute of Economy, Trade, and Industry (RIETI). We are grateful to all the participant in the study group for useful discussions. The second author gratefully acknowledges the financial support of a Grant-in-Aid for Scientific Research (A) (#16H02015) from the Japan Society for the Promotion of Science.

S. Pu
Taraxa, San Jose, CA, USA

M. Yano (✉)
Research Institute of Economy, Trade and Industry (RIETI), Tokyo, Japan
e-mail: yano-makoto@rieti.go.jp

M. Yano et al. (eds.), *Blockchain and Crypto Currency*,
Economics, Law, and Institutions in Asia Pacific,
https://doi.org/10.1007/978-981-15-3376-1_2

Few would disagree that a tight-knit IoT-based society is just around the corner. However, this does not imply that a "human-centered" smart society like that envisioned by Society 5.0 will be realized automatically.

To obtain Society 5.0, it is necessary to build a new ecosystem in which data collected through the IoT can be utilized in an efficient and fair manner through high quality markets.[2] Many worry about the possibility that a large number of jobs could be lost to AI (see Acemoglu and Restrepo 2018; Yano and Furukawa 2019), including the eminent physicist Stephen Hawking, and some even argue that someday humans will be controlled by AI (see Kharpal 2017). Although these worries may reflect the irrational fear of a poorly understood technology that could drastically change our society, there is a more immediate concern that may underlie this fear.

That concern is the mishandling and misappropriation of big data, which many people perceive to be posing a serious threat to the present society. For example, the recent Cambridge Analytica scandal has revealed that the phishing and mishandling of personal data that are collected digitally through a social media company such as Facebook may pose a grave threat to modern society by polarizing people's views on sociopolitical issues.[3] Unless these challenges are overcome, the human-centered smart society can never be realized.

It is our view that these problems have emerged because the ownership of data collected through the Internet is not clearly defined. As a result, a seemingly unlimited volume of data is collected freely by large Internet companies. The Cambridge Analytica case suggests that such data can be easily abused.

This study demonstrates that blockchain is a key to achieving Society 5.0 by creating a high quality market for IoT big data, in which data are used both efficiently and fairly. The obstacles standing in front of this goal stem from a lack of proper ownership of big data generated through the IoT.

Blockchain is a perfect mechanism to record the ownership of scarce resources. This is because blockchain is a ledger; as Webster (1961) explains, a ledger is "a book of permanent record." It was initially developed to create a secure, decentralized digital record on the Internet to keep track of ownership of credits and debts and their changes over time. If blockchain can make a secure record for the ownership of IoT big data, a question remains as to who should own IoT big data: the immediate party who generated the data, or that who collected the data?

As shown below, market quality theory implies that it is desirable to assign the ownership of IoT big data to the immediate party who generated the data rather than that who collected the data. That would prevent the development of large data monopolies, thereby making it possible to utilize economically valuable IoT big data in a more efficient and fairer manner.

---

[2]The concept of fairness here is that developed by Yano's market quality theory (Yano 2009, 2017, 2019).

[3]According to a recent *Guardian* article (Cadwalladr 2018), Cambridge Analytica illegally created psychological profiles of 230 million Americans, which it used to influence various elections, including the 2016 Brexit referendum and the 2016 U.S. Presidential election.

To handle IoT big data in a blockchain, it is necessary to have a new blockchain on which smart contracts can be executed. A smart contract is a computer program that executes software commands in the way in which the smart contract stipulates for each contingency. It therefore minimizes the cost of dispute resolutions that a usual contract would have to bear; in the case of a standard contract, a dispute is usually resolved by a court. This, however, does not imply that a blockchain eliminates all possible disputes; those that cannot be resolved within a blockchain system must be resolved in the light of relevant laws to ensure the operational viability and quality of an IoT data market.

In what follows, we explain the uses of IoT in Sect. 2. Section 3 shows that IoT big data are underutilized due to data security concerns and data monopoly. In Sect. 4, we explain that blockchain could alleviate these problems by assigning the ownership of IoT big data to the individuals who create data through their daily activities. Section 5 explains market quality theory, which gives an analytical basis for this chapter. In Sect. 6, we explain from the viewpoint of market quality theory why the ownership of IoT big data should be assigned to the individual data producers but not to the platform companies that collect data. Section 6 also covers potential issues that IoT blockchains may face in the future.

2 IoT in Society 5.0

IoT connects cyberspace and physical space, providing the foundation for Society 5.0. Society 5.0, pushed by the Japanese government's Fifth Science and Technology Basic Plan (2016–2020), refers to an image of a near-future society in which cyberspace (virtual space) and physical space (real space) are completely integrated. It is perceived as the upgrade of the previous version of a society, Society 4.0, in which "people would access a cloud service (databases) in cyberspace via the Internet and search for, retrieve, and analyze information or data." Society 5.0 envisions a society that will come out of the Fourth Industrial Revolution, in which a large volume of data (big data) can be made available via the Internet with the use of sensors attached to objects in physical space and will accumulate in cyberspace. In cyberspace, in turn, the data will be analyzed by AI, and the resulting data will be fed back to humans.

IoT is a network of physical components such as devices, tools, machines, home appliances, and even people that are connected via the Internet to one another. Sensors are attached to each of those components; data collected by sensors can be accessed through the Internet.

People are also a part of the IoT network through smart phones. Everyone who owns a smartphone is digitally coded by a telephone number. A variety of applications are incorporated into a smartphone, creating huge volumes of personal data. For example, people use the iPhone camera to take pictures not just for fun but also for records and analyses; most repairmen use smartphones to take pictures of what they are supposed to fix. This information is sent not only to their offices but also to parts manufacturers, who can analyze the problem to come up with proper solutions. This is precisely what IoT is supposed to achieve: the collection of data via sensors integrated inside devices (camera in the above example), communication of the data through the Internet, analysis of the data as required, and identification of suitable solutions.

Humans are attached to many other IoT sensors. Pedometers, which are used to count the number of steps that a person makes by walking, are now equipped with rather sophisticated sensors. They not only record the number of steps but also monitor physical motion, heart beat, calories burnt, and even how one sleeps—REM, light, deep sleep, and awake periods. These data are communicated to the manufacturers, who analyze the data and then provide various pieces of advice for you to live a healthier life.

IoT is used for more serious situations as well. In every corner of a city, we see automated external defibrillators, which externally administer electric shocks to one's heart to eliminate life-threatening fibrillations. This device is now put into pacemakers that are implanted in patients with serious cardiac conditions; whenever fibrillations occur, the pacemaker catches the signal and gives internal electric shocks to the heart to realign the heartbeat. At every moment, data can be collected by the pacemaker and sent through the Internet to doctors and manufacturers who constantly monitor the patients and their pacemakers.[4]

IoT is also important for taking care of people who need assistance from others; as the society becomes wealthier, the importance of care for the elderly, child care, and patient care will increase. Alzheimer's patients who lose short-term memory need assistance with cognitively demanding tasks. For example, they are more likely to forget simple tasks that can have consequences for health and safety, particularly related to cooking. Such scenarios have always required the constant supervision of a relative or carer. IoT devices will be able to replace some of these human chores. A house can be wired to the Internet with motion sensors, which can track movement in the different rooms and areas of the house. With these sensors, families and health service companies can monitor when the patient wakes up, goes to the kitchen, and so on.

Perhaps one of the most important industrial applications of IoT may be in the agricultural sector. The IoT provides a new method of agricultural production. Sensors can be attached to livestock to collect health and growth data through the Internet, which can be used to control the administration of feed and medicine. Every square meter of farmland can be monitored by sensors that collect agricultural data, for example, soil moisture, fertilizer density, sunshine, temperature, and so on, and send them through either wireless or wired networks to a control center. The control center can then analyze data and optimize the use of agricultural input to external environments. This application of IoT can optimize the use and cost of expensive fertilizer and pesticide, because the IoT sensors can detect exactly which parts of the field, and how much, plants need to be fertilized or treated with pesticides. Agriculture is

[4]In many cases, data from a pacemaker is first sent via a smartphone to a base station for security reasons. One can imagine what could happen if a pacemaker network were overtaken by individuals with malicious intent.

highly water intensive. When water is supplied by sprinklers, a significant portion of water never reaches the plants because of evaporation. The use of IoT to monitor the soil moisture and to optimize the water supply to each small area of farmland would greatly economize water usage. This capability will become increasingly important as global warming continues.

Another important application of IoT relates to cars, particularly for the development of self-driving cars, which simply could not function without IoT. Self-driving cars use many sensors, including high-quality radars and cameras, to map out the car's surroundings. The IoT system processes the feedback from the sensors, calculates a path to take, and gives directions to the car's controls. Cars are equipped with mechanisms to avoid obstacles, obey traffic rules, and minimize damage in case of an unavoidable accident. While we may have to wait a long time before driverless cars become widely used, there are more immediate applications of IoT in cars. It can collect data on the working status of various vital parts of cars, which can then be analyzed to contribute to safer driving. IoT can also gather information on driving habits and analyze data for safer driving, and could provide vital risk information to insurance companies.

The Japanese government designated Society 5.0 as a national goal, creating a society where "people, things, and systems are all connected in cyberspace and optimal results obtained by AI exceeding the capabilities of humans are fed back to physical space. This process brings new value to industry and society in ways not previously possible." To achieve this goal, as discussed below, it is highly important to fully utilize data collected in the IoT space.

All economists would agree that the best way to make efficient use of scarce resources is to rely on the market. IoT data is no exception. It has been known in economics that the establishment of private ownership for resources is a prerequisite for the development of a market for those resources (see Coase 1960). In reality, however, the ownership of data collected via the Internet has not yet been clearly established. Yano's market quality theory implies that Society 5.0 would be unrealizable without high-quality markets (see Yano 2009). Although healthy competitive environments are a prerequisite for a high-quality market, data produced through Internet transactions are currently monopolized by a few gigantic Internet companies, including Google, Amazon, and Facebook. As we discuss below, new types of blockchain may break data monopoly and bring the economic use of data into a competitive environment.

3 IoT Big Data: Underutilization, Unfairness, and Inefficiency

As we watch science fiction movies, we see a future filled with autonomous devices flying around, doing things on their own accord, and constantly trading information and data. That is a great vision. The sad truth is, however, that we are still very far from such a future.

The IoT space has not really moved forward in substantive ways, at least not in the past one or two decades. IoT investments today largely consist of infrastructural hardware and software, but what really makes IoT valuable is the enormous amount of data they collect. If the data cannot be effectively utilized, the devices and the infrastructure are useless and their investment is unjustifiable. As of this writing, only a small sliver of data is actually being put to use, while the rest languish in data silos. Only when we start taking full advantage of this data can we truly realize the potential of IoT.

Application discovery has always been difficult, which is why healthy ecosystems require the broadest participation possible to maximize the chances of discovering viable applications. IoT systems, on the other hand, are invariably closed, as manufacturers, systems integrators, and owners of these systems build up layers upon layers of walled gardens denying access to their data, despite the fact that the data is not close to being fully leveraged or monetized.

Hence, one of the most fundamental challenges facing the IoT space today is the lack of sharing and trading of IoT data. Without it, broad participation cannot be achieved, and data will remain fragmented and useless. But why is it so hard to trade data or to share data? As we discuss below, this may be attributed to two factors: data security and data monopolization.

3.1 Data Security Issues

Why is IoT big data not fully utilized? The first reason relates to data security and privacy concerns, where people are afraid that they will be unfairly treated. If data is lost or stolen, devices can be compromised and secret information could be leaked.

The second reason is driven by business and economic considerations. Why should this data be collected? How could money be made from this data? If no compelling business goals or business models can be articulated, there will be no way to persuade people or companies to make investments. The problem of high cost must also be considered. The cost of IoT is not just incurred in the purchase of a sensor. It includes the connectivity cost, the storage cost, and the analytics cost. There are many hidden costs involved with IoT, and if the investment cannot be justified with reasonable returns, the investment will not be made.

A third reason for a lack of data utilization is insufficient internal expertise, which creates a fear of vendor lock-in. Because most companies do not really have the expertise to analyze data, they tend to outsource the task to a third party. However, companies may also have concerns for their own privacy; sharing data with an external platform or vendor not only reveals information to outsiders, but the company may also become overly reliant upon these external partners, leading to loss of control and potentially creating new competitors. Such sentiments are strong, which further prevents companies from sharing data.

As discussed above, blockchain technology is designed to provide secure records and permissions. It is therefore expected to greatly reduce the mishandling and monopolization of big data, which many people perceive as posing a serious threat to the society.

As news of problems like the Cambridge Analytica scandal spread, more and more people are turning to blockchain, which makes it possible to share and distribute data in a secure fashion. For example, IBM has introduced an IoT blockchain service, which makes it possible "to send data to private blockchain ledgers for inclusion in shared transactions with tamper-resistant records."[5] However, the problem cannot be fully resolved by ensuring just data security.

3.2 Data Monopoly Issues

The monopolization of big data by the large platform companies presents challenges to effective data utilization. Some fear a serious threat to democracy, bringing the digital economy to a "winner-takes-all arena, with a small number of companies controlling large parts of the market" (Cerf et al. 2018). Such a consideration is said to underlie the recent adoption of the General Data Protection Regulation of the EU (Cable 2018). Khan (2016) argues that platform companies like Amazon exploit their scope to engage in predatory pricing; according to a recent article in the *New York Times*, her argument has been well received among policymakers and has started to influence antitrust laws.[6]

The fundamental reason why data monopolies have formed in the recent economy is the lack of proper data ownership. This is no surprise given that big data did not even exist until very recently. Except for very limited types of data, there had been no way to either collect or use data.

To consider how personal data has been used in commerce in the past, suppose that you have just purchased Karl Marx's classic book *Das Kapital* at your local book store. From this piece of data, the book store can deduce that you are likely to be an economist. You are probably liberal in the political spectrum and highly educated (the book is rather difficult to read). A single piece of data like this is therefore useful for a bookstore to give a personalized advice and recommendations to a customer. This used to be the type of service that local book stores provided years ago. The economic value of that piece of data was so small that no one tried to claim the ownership; it is safe to assume that such data were implicitly co-owned by bookstores and their customers.

The Internet has completely changed the nature of personal data of this sort; online vendors can now collect extremely large volumes of data with minimal cost. Such data are highly valuable because many different statistical predictions can be

---

[5]See https://www.ibm.com/Internet-of-things/spotlight/blockchain.

[6]Also see the *New York Times* article introducing Khan's work (Streitfeld 2018).

made with respect to different groups of people; one example is the way in which Cambridge Analytica has used stolen data.[7]

As a result, gigantic data monopolies have been created in which the ownership has been claimed by default as data accumulate in the server. This has occurred even before the society can agree on who owns Internet data, which has perhaps contributed to the current sentiment against big data monopolies.

4 Decentralization: Towards Fair and Efficient Use

Perhaps the most important innovation that blockchain can bring into IoT space is the distributed ownership of data created by the IoT. Through blockchain technology, all data generated by IoT devices can be encrypted. Each piece of encrypted data can be signed by the private key of the device that generates that piece of data. This means that blockchain technology makes it possible for the owner of the device generating a particular piece of data to own that very piece.

As discussed below, blockchain could greatly alleviate the unfair and inefficient utilization of big data by assigning the ownership of each single piece of data generated by the IoT to the person who generates the data. In expanding the IoT, smartphones will play an important role as IoT devices in collecting big data. To assign decentralized private ownership and put it to widespread use, a new blockchain needs to be developed that is tailored to the decentralization of IoT data ownership.

4.1 Unfair Data Monopoly

Right now, more and more people feel that big data are unfairly collected. To see people's frustrations, it is useful to digress briefly and consider the social media industry, which is one generation older than the IoT big data industry. Reflecting their feeling of unfairness, people have started developing social media networks based on blockchain.

Information is free. It creates invaluable external benefits to society. This is the general perception that has greatly helped the development of social media companies. People are connected to their friends from totally different regions of the world through social media; a lot of personal information from different parts of the world is exchanged instantaneously. Active interactions of people helps to deepen their mutual understanding and even the cross-cultural understanding of each other. This brings the world closer and helps to create a more human-centered, friendly society.

Such network externality-based considerations have long supported the development of social media services. However, as several social media companies have

[7] In the recent literature, it has been established that people's opinions and views can be critically influenced by the way in which information is presented. For example, see Horiuchi and Ono (2018).

grown into huge network platform monopolies, many people have started to question the ethics of such data monopolies.

Why do people willingly give up their personal data to large social media companies, which can use the data in anyway they want to make profits? This appears quite unfair. As the Cambridge Analytica scandal shows, this practice can lead to the misappropriation of personal data. That is undoubtedly a dirty trick, so it is not surprising that a large number of people are bothered by unfair operational protocols that social media companies like to enforce.

This change reflects a change in the nature of a monopolistic market, as network platform monopolies grow. In the market, multiple network platform companies compete with one another. However, the information and data that a particular company has collected is now locked into that company, which can act as a monopoly with entry barriers made up of its data. This has resulted in a new monopolistic market that appears to be completely different from conventional monopolistic market like the late 19th century oil industry, which was dominated by Standard Oil. In the oil market, the products traded are uniform, whereas in the present network platform market, each platform company offers its own unique service.

A similar market structure is called monopolistic competition in economics. Under monopolistic competition, as in the market for wine, many companies supply their own unique differentiated products in competition. Dominated by far fewer and much larger network platform companies, the social media market differs from a typical monopolistically competitive market.

As noted above, blockchain technology provides a way to challenge such a data monopoly. An Ethereum-based platform called Indorse (https://indorse.io/) is a good example.

Indorse is a social media network for IT professionals, which adopts a decentralized consensus mechanism. That is, in submitting the portfolio of one's professional skills, it is evaluated by other random professionals in the network. When an individual uses the site, he/she is asked to choose his/her skills from JavaScript, Java, Solidity, Python, and C#. The submission is then evaluated by others and published on the Indorse network in a secure manner. Anyone who submits personal data for skills evaluation will receive some units of token that can be used for services like advertising and company pages with validated connections. Indorse explains that in this way, the cost of professional accreditation can be economized, that the lack of skillful evaluators for emerging and soft skills can be alleviated, and that possible bias and fraud that may occur with professional accreditation can be minimized.

4.2 *Inefficient Use of IoT Big Data*

Blockchain can ameliorate the underutilization of big data in many ways. First, it is based on a decentralized operating model. Because it is a decentralized network, users are not dependent upon any single entity. Everyone runs his/her own node.[8] Thus, everyone can be independent, which prevents data monopoly. Everyone is decentralized. Thus, no one is being locked into any one platform or set of infrastructures.

Second, blockchain could significantly lower a rather high entry barrier into the network platform industry. There are several factors that makes it difficult for newcomers to compete against established big companies. Think of YouTube, for example. The first issue is the brand. Everyone knows, uses, and likes YouTube. Many people watch it almost habitually. Once people start accepting a particular service at that level, a brand name is established, which is one layer of competitive advantage. The second factor is the data and algorithms that form a virtuous cycle that allows YouTube to become increasingly accurate in their content categorization, targeting, and advertising. The third is the infrastructure that the company has built. It has servers, it has technology, and it has negotiated great contracts with Internet service providers to make sure it enjoys prioritized traffic routing. All of this established infrastructure is difficult to replicate. Even if someone were to spend billions of dollars to replicate it, one could fail easily. Blockchain significantly weakens the second and third parts of the competitive barrier by decentralizing the data, algorithms, and eventually the hardware infrastructure, turning them into commodities accessible by anyone. As Yano (2019) shows, one source of market power is the bundling of commodities. If someone can bundle up commodities into a big chunk, they can exercise bargaining power over trading partners and force them to accept unfavorable terms of trade. As discussed above, that is precisely what is happening in the current data market.

Third, blockchain fractionalizes resources into pieces, which could drastically increase the number of people who participate in the IoT big data market. Data will become increasingly open-source, which removes the intellectual property barrier. Storage, processing power, and connectivity are all fractionalized, and can be used on a decentralized network. If that is achieved, anybody will be able to replicate the structure of entities like YouTube over night. Then, the existing brand barrier will also be reduced. Many different products will be tested on the market and those that are deemed truly valuable will be accepted as new brands. Of course, existing brands like YouTube can compete with these new products; if they prove valuable, they will remain in the market.

Fourth, blockchain would stimulate big data usage by enabling each individual to sell data that he/she generates at the same time to buy data that he/she needs. Right now, except for a few data monopolies, everyone has to participate in the big data market as a buyer even though he/she is also a producer of data. The decentralization of data ownership would lead to a perfectly competitive market for big data in which everyone can participate in data transactions in two ways: as a seller of the data he/she produces and as a buyer of the data that others produce. In a society in which cyberspace and physical space are integrated, everyone would become a supplier of data at the same time that he/she could act as a demander of data. If blockchain

[8] A node implies a participant on the network. Often it is an Internet/computer account through which one obtains access to a network as well as keeping a local copy of the entire network data.

would make it possible to create a market in which all sorts of data are traded, the data usage would become much more efficient than in the market where everyone has to participate as a buyer except a few data monopolists, who can manipulate the types of data to supply. In history, many mechanisms have been developed that make it possible for people to share ownership of an asset: corporate stocks and bonds, securitization of debts and other obligations, time-share of a second house, and rental cars. These mechanisms all help to utilize resources more efficiently. As discussed above, blockchain is one such mechanism that enables sharing small pieces of data. This provides an important way to challenge data monopolies owned by large platform companies and to promote more efficient usage of data where anyone can participate.

Fifth, the use of blockchain to decentralize data ownership would promote technological innovations, which cannot be expected from monopolies. Although an enormous volume of data has been accumulated at big platform companies, it is likely that much of the data has not been utilized. This is because it is beyond a single entity's capability to understand the full spectrum of all potential applications in the world. For a large company with a great deal of data, it is typical to acquire external expertise through requests for proposal. However, even if a company employs external resources, it is still unlikely that they can cover the full spectrum all possible applications. This is why a decentralized network where any entity can participate will effectively and hugely expand the amount of external expertise that any single entity can access.

More broadly, the idea of involving external resources by a decentralized network relates to open-source and open-innovation initiatives, which are pushed forward by many policymakers all over the world.[9] Many people say that because they cannot find a business case for this data, they are not going to use it. If, however, data are released to an open community, it is certain that some will figure out what to do with it.

Because blockchain is a public ledger on a decentralized open network, anyone can join. This implies that blockchain encourages competition. In the future data market, the idea of competitive advantage will become much less important. Competition will become much fairer and will occur on an equal footing.

4.3 Decentralized Creation

To build a blockchain for an IoT network, smartphones are expected to play an important role. To this end, Apple has made a big contribution to the decentralization of data by allowing all data that is being generated by iPhone, an IoT device, to be released to the public. Anyone can build any application on top of it, leverage the data, and leverage the device. That has made Apple hugely valuable. If Apple were to have monopolized all data, it would be worth a small fraction of what it is worth

[9]For recent issues on open innovation, see Bogers et al. (2018).

today. Because it made the conscious decision to share and open up the data created by this IoT device, iPhone and Apple have become highly valuable.

From the viewpoint of data usage, iPhone is the most successful IoT device in history. This is because of the conscious decision of Apple to open up the Apple Store, which has made iPhone hugely successful. Through iPhone, many types of data have been collected in large volumes. The device is equipped with many different sensors such as gyroscope, compass, barometer, and camera and all collect data whenever iPhone is used.

4.4 Need for a New Blockchain Protocol to Handle IoT Data

Most of the IoT data is big data, which is far beyond the scope of the original blockchain for Bitcoin. As Omote and Yano (2020) explain, the Bitcoin blockchain is designed to handle numerical data on transactions, each piece of which is rather small.

Ethereum is also unable to handle IoT big data. It is a classic linear blockchain built on the Bitcoin system. Because of this, two weak points arise. First, it is built on a wasteful system. If 10,000 nodes are generating blocks, the work of 9999 will be wasted; only one node can win. That concept is very wasteful. Second, it is very slow. Every single moment, Ethereum works on a single node in sequence; if a large number of transactions are waiting to be included in the chain, they have to line up to wait for their respective turns. These weak points can easily create a serious bottleneck for Ethereum.

For fullutilization of IoT big data, something far beyond these classic blockchains is required. The concept of concurrent smart contracts is one idea to deal with this problem.

As explained by Yano et al. (2020), "a smart contract is a computerized transaction protocol that executes the terms of a contract." [It is supposed to] satisfy "common contractual conditions (such as payment terms, liens, confidentiality, and even enforcement), [to] minimize exceptions both malicious and accidental, and [to] minimize the need for trusted intermediaries" (Szabo 1994). The blockchain for Bitcoin can handle incomplete smart contracts only in the sense that it produces a record of payments.

A more complete smart contract adds a layer of logic on top of the Bitcoin blockchain In this case, the smart contract is essentially a program. Ethereum adds the function of executing a complete program on top of the Bitcoin type blockchain. Ethereum adds this function to the blockchain for Bitcoin.

For example, a smart contract can incorporate a voting mechanism. Who likes this TV program? People can vote on such an issue. A smart contract can create a voting mechanism by which the results of the votes are all encoded into the blockchain. Then, the votes become immutable and fully transparent, which the classic blockchain ensures.

On Ethereum, the smart contract size is theoretically unlimited. However, it is costly to execute a smart contract on Ethereum because one has to pay to store and process smart contract s. This fee structure effectively sets an upper limit on the size of a smart contract on Ethereum, which makes it costly to write a sophisticated program (smart contract) that needs to handle IoT big data freely.

To overcome this problem, a new protocol is desirable. A "concurrent small contract" occurs when under any single node, the node is able to process hundreds of smart contract calls simultaneously. It uses theory called software transactional memory, which does speculative parallelization of smart contract costs. In the next chapter, Steven Pu explains this in detail.

5 Market Quality: Fairness and Efficiency

So far, the terms efficiency and fairness have been used without explaining their precise meaning. Efficiency is a standard economic concept, which might need no explanation; it refers to a state in which the right resources are allocated to the right places. Fairness, in contrast, is a new concept, and was introduced as competitive fairness in Yano (2008). It is a new concept of economics, and was introduced as a normative measure for the performance of a market. See Yano (2019) for precise definitions of fairness and market quality.

5.1 Market Quality Theory

Yano (2009) defines market quality as a normative measure that reflects both efficiency and competitive fairness. With this concept, Yano's market quality theory can be summarized by the following two propositions:

First Proposition: High- quality markets are indispensable for healthy economic growth.

Second Proposition: Well-developed market infrastructure is indispensable for maintaining high-quality markets.

These two propositions are drawn from the observation that we have experienced three large and rapid technological advances, which are often referred to as industrial revolutions. These industrial revolutions resulted in significant declines in market quality. Once the disrupting effect of an industrial revolution subsided, market quality went back up, thereby leading to the next industrial revolution. This process is illustrated by the three C curves in Fig. 1 Market quality may be characterized by three different factors: the quality of competition, the quality of information, and the quality of goods. The lowering of market quality in each of the three C curves may be associated with these factors.

The First Industrial Revolution began with the invention of the steam engine in eighteenth-century England. Right after this period, the quality of the labor market

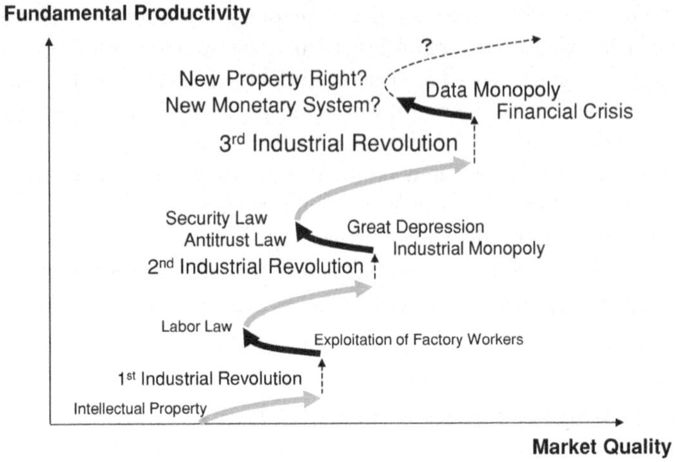

Fig. 1 Market quality dynamics

fell; it is well known that this experience led to the Marxian theory of labor exploitation (Marx 1867). As Yano (2005) shows, labor exploitation can occur when the quality of competition falls.

The Second Industrial Revolution was spread over a relatively long period. It started with the invention of the Bessemer converter for steel production in the mid-1850s, which drastically lowered the steel price and led to a construction boom of railroads, bridges, and steel ships. In the mid-1870s, the economy contracted sharply and fell into a long period of stagnation, which lasted until the early 1890s; this stagnation was so severe that it was called the Long Depression. During the period of stagnation, large monopolies, as represented by Standard Oil, developed. This was considered to have a serious negative impact on the society and led to the antitrust law of 1890 in the USA. The other technological advance during the Second Industrial Revolution was the use of electrical power during the turn of the century. This period of rapid growth ended with the Great Depression of the 1930s. The US congress perceived the Great Depression as a result of mishandling and misappropriation (or the lowering of quality) of information in securities markets, which led to the Securities Act of 1933. It is generally perceived that a lowering of the quality of information in the securities market caused the Long Depression and the Great Depression.

The technological progress that we have experienced in information and communication technology since the 1990s may be thought of as the Third Industrial Revolution, which may have been a major player in bringing about the 2008 global financial crisis; Yano (2010) explains this as a result of the lowering of the quality of securities.

5.2 Competitive Fairness

There is no doubt that "good markets" and "bad markets" exist in the real world. Few buyers would disagree that a good market is a market in which better products are available for a lower price. Indeed, no other answer expresses the nature of a good market quite so accurately for a buyer. If you are a seller, however, the opposite is true. In other words, from the seller's point of view, a good market is a market in which you can sell better products for more. In general, there is a range of price that is determined by balancing the needs and desires of buyers and sellers. Unless a price is set in this range, it cannot be considered to be appropriate.

If prices are set in an appropriate range, it is often a result of competitively unfair transactions. According to the Unabridged Edition of Merriam-Webster (1961), competition is "the act or action of seeking to gain what another is seeking to gain at the same time and usually under or as if under fair or equitable rules and circumstances." Moreover, "fair" refers to a state "conforming to an established commonly accepted code or the rules of a game or other competitive activities." These definitions attest to the importance of fairness for a market, which cannot function without competition. The concept of market quality follows this idea.

Yano (2008, 2009) defines that market actions and activities are competitively fair (or simply fair) if they are conducted in compliance with the following fundamental rules.[10]

Rule 1 (private property right): Goods traded in the market must be subject to transferable private ownership.

Rule 2 (voluntary action): Transactions in the market must be voluntary.

Rule 3 (nondiscrimination):

1. Third-party individuals and direct trading partners must be treated equally.
2. Anyone can freely trade with anyone in any amount or, more broadly, on any terms.

The protection of private properties (Rule 1) is perhaps one of the most fundamental rules for a human society, which is evidenced by one of the Ten Commandments "You shall not steal." In economics, the role of this rule has been studied extensively since the work of Coase (1960). His fundamental conclusion, known as the Coase theorem, implies that unless proper property rights are established for resources, the market for those resources cannot develop. This theorem gave a basic theoretical framework in which issues such as externalities and torts are analyzed in economic terms. The same consideration motivates the present study, focusing on the ownership of IoT big data.

The protection of voluntary actions (Rule 2) is also a basic rule that supports a civil society. In economics, the importance of this rule has been recognized since the work of Smith (1776), referring to the invisible hand. Subsequently, Smith's theory

[10]Yano (2009) includes the equal treatment under rules as the fourth fundamental rule. The rules presented above follows Yano (2019).

has been elaborated by many studies including Edgeworth (1883) and Debreu and Scarf (1963).

The nondiscriminatory treatment of Rule 3 can be traced back to Chapter 41 of the Magna Carta (1215), which had influence on the early development of US property commercial codes during the American Revolution period (Hulsebosch 2016). As Yano (2008) demonstrates, the US corporate law, in particular, on mergers and acquisitions is in line with Rule 3, which is interpreted to stipulate that no one is allowed to discriminate one trading partner from another for noneconomic terms.

6 Creation of a High-Quality Big Data Market

As discussed in Sect. 4, we argue that the ownership of data should be assigned to the person who generates the data, which can be made possible by a properly designed blockchain technology. Before closing this chapter, we explain this conclusion from the viewpoint of market quality theory.

6.1 Assignment of Data Ownership

Market quality theory implies that the ownership of a scarce resource should be established in such a way that it may lead to the creation of a market with higher quality. This conclusion is an extension of the Coase theorem (Coase 1960).

The theorem implies that the market for particular resources cannot develop before the transferable ownership is established with respect to those resources. Once proper ownership is assigned, incentives for trade will be created, thereby forming a market in a decentralized manner. The working of market mechanism is neutral to the way in which the ownership is assigned if market transactions are not costly (neutrality result). If transaction costs are not negligible, the ownership should be established in such a way that a more efficient allocation can be reached in the resulting market.

As Khan (2016) points out, network platform companies like Amazon provide highly competitive services at low prices, which implies plentiful supply. In other words, the market for network platform services is rather efficient. If we assume that the IoT big data market is to develop into a similar market structure, the Coase theorem is of little use for the determination of data ownership.

Khan (2016) proposes that the antitrust law, evaluating predatory pricing, should depart from the price theory-based approach and shift back to the old structuralism, analyzing the "competitive process and market structure" (Khan 2016 p. 745). She then lists "a range of factors that give insight into the neutrality of the competitive process and the openness of the market," [which include] entry barriers, conflicts of interest, the emergence of gatekeepers or bottlenecks, the use of and control over data, and the dynamics of bargaining power. Such a categorical approach to the antitrust law is, however, dangerous for the healthy growth of ever-changing markets such as those for IoT big data, blockchain, and social media, which is probably why the US court has shifted away from structuralism.

6.2 *Predatory Pricing and Exploitation: A Price Theory Approach*

Market quality theory provides a price theoretical basis for predatory pricing and exploitation. Under the nondiscrimination rule (Rule 3), as discussed above, no one should be locked into trading with a particular trading partner. If one receives a better offer than anything from the current trading partner, he/she should be free to move to take the new offer.

As Yano (2008) demonstrates, the nondiscrimination rule ensures every market participant a surplus at least as large as that which the best outside offer (or alternative competitive offer) avails. Even if one trades with a monopoly, it should receive such a surplus, which he/she could receive if a transaction were made in a competitive environment. As Yano (2005) shows, this result gives an economic explanation to the real world cases of predatory pricing and economic exploitation, which has not been treated in the previous economic literature.[11]

This study has pointed out several potential problems in the case in which the ownership of IoT big data is assigned to the companies that collect data. First of all, it is likely that large data monopolies like the current network platform companies would be formed. Such a monopoly could abuse monopoly power, which has been observed in social media companies. Moreover, big data might not be shared and traded efficiently in a market; underutilization of valuable data could result. All these factors reduce the quality of an IoT big data market. In short, market quality theory stipulates that the ownership of IoT big data should be assigned to those who generate data by themselves, which is made possible by blockchain technology.

6.3 *Further Discussions*

A market filled with contractual disputes cannot be regarded as being high quality; such disputes arise when, in a very basic sense, some of the three fundamental rules above are violated. Combined with the idea of a smart contract, blockchain technology introduces a completely new way in which social obligations are enforced. In modern society, many social obligations are enforced centrally by laws. In a smart contract, in contrast, transactions are enforced by computer algorithm, which can be

[11] For example, see Khan (2016), who points out that under the current framework of antitrust law, which is based on efficiency, output, and prices, it is difficult to "cognize the potential harms to competition by Amazon's dominance."

expected to wipe out any contractual disputes. This, however, does not imply that the contractual arrangements in a blockchain are free from dispute.

There are many potential sources of dispute in the transactions of IoT big data. This may be explained by using the example of Indorse, a decentralized social media network for IT professionals. In this blockchain, a particular applicant's professional skills are evaluated by peers and securely published in the blockchain. If participants are all honest, the smart contract in the blockchain would create a valuable dataset for IT professionals, which all potential clients and employers can rely on. If, however, dishonest individuals starts submitting fake portfolios, it would no longer be the case. In that case, whether a particular person's skill set posted in the blockchain network is reliable must be decided outside of the network; one obvious way to check the reliability is simply to interview a candidate before deciding to hire. If the fraction of dishonest individuals increases, even interviewing would become too costly, in which case the network itself would become useless.

A deeper problem would arise if a potential employer were to suffer significant damage or loss by employing a dishonest individual. The employer would find it difficult to claim compensation for the damage against the network, which is built in a decentralized manner with no one explicitly responsible.

From an economic viewpoint, such a problem can be expected to be eliminated in the long run because people would cease to rely on an erratic network. In the interim, however, dishonest individuals may pose a serious problem. To avoid such problems, it is important to maintain competitive fairness in the sense of market quality theory.

References

Acemoglu D, Restrepo P (2018) The race between man and machine: implications of technology for growth, factor shares, and employment. Am Econ Rev 108–6:1488–1542

Bogers M, Chesbrough H, Moedas C (2018) Open innovation: research, practice, and policies. Calif Manage Rev 60(2):5–16. https://doi.org/10.1177/0008125617745086

Cable V (2018) The tech titans must have their monopoly broken—and this is how we do it. The Guardian, Apr. 20, 2018. https://www.theguardian.com/commentisfree/2018/apr/20/tech-monopoly-apple-facebook-data-extreme-content

Cadwalladr C (2018) 'I made Steve Bannon's psychological warfare tool': meet the data war whistleblower. The Guardian, Mar. 13, 2018. https://www.theguardian.com/news/2018/mar/17/data-war-whistleblower-christopher-wylie-faceook-nix-bannon-trump

Cerf M, Matz S, Rolnik G (2018) Commentary: there's still time to stop the tech monopoly takeover. Forbus, Mar. 8, 2018

Coase R (1960) The problem of social cost. J Law Econ 3(1): 1–44. https://doi.org/10.1086/466560

Debreu G, Scarf H (1963) A limit theorem on the core of an economy. Int Econ Rev 4(3):235–246

Edgeworth F (1883) Mathematical psychics. London

Horiuchi Y, Ono Y (2018) Public opposition to refugee resettlement: the case of Japan. RIETI Discussion paper series 18-E-050, Japan

Hulsebosch, D (2016) Magna carta for the world: the merchant's chapter and foreign capital in the early American Republic, 94 N.C. L. Rev. 1599

Khan LM (2016) Amazon's antitrust paradox. Yale Law J 126(3):710–805

Kharpal A (2017) Stephen hawking says A.I. could be 'worst event in the history of our civilization'. CNBC, Nov 6, 2017
Marx K (1867) Das Kapital, vol. 1
Omote K, Yano M (2020) Bitcoin and Blockchain Technology. mimeo. RIETI
Smith A (1776) Wealth of nations
Streitfeld D (2018) Amazon's antitrust antagonist has a breakthrough idea. New York Times, Sept 7, 2018. https://www.nytimes.com/2018/09/07/technology/monopoly-antitrust-lina-khan-amazon.html
Szabo N (1994) Smart contracts. http://www.fon.hum.uva.nl/rob/Courses/InformationInSpeech/CDROM/Literature/LOTwinterschool2006/szabo.best.vwh.net/smart.contracts.html
Webster (1961). Webster's third new international dictionary of the English Language, Unabridged, 3rd revised ed, Merriam-Webster
Yano M (2005) Shitsu no Jidai no System Kaikaku (System reform in the era of quality). Iwanami, Tokyo
Yano M (2008) Competitive fairness and the concept of a fair price under delaware law on M&A. Int J Econ Theor 4–2(175–190):2008
Yano M (2009) The foundation of market quality economics. Japan Econ Rev 60–1(1–32):2009
Yano M (2010) The 2008 world financial crisis and market quality theory. Asian Econ Pap 9(3):172–192
Yano M (2017) Law and economics on market quality. RIETI Highlight 63:2–6
Yano M (2019) Market quality theory and the Coase theorem in the presence of transaction costs. RIETI Discussion paper series 19-E-097
Yano M, Furukawa Y (2019) Economic black holes and total job destruction in the presence of self-replicating artificial intelligence. RIETI Discussion papers 19062
Yano M, Dai C, Masuda K, Kishimoto Y (2020) Blockchain business and its regulation. mimeo. RIETI

Steven Pu is an entrepreneur and strategy consultant. Prior to founding Taraxa, he co-founded multiple venture-funded startups in wireless mesh networks, mobile health, and healthcare services. He was also a director at Monitor Deloitte's China office, spearheading the firm's digital strategy practice, advising senior executives of multinational corporations on how large organizations could effectively capture innovation and respond quickly to market disruptions.

Mr. Pu holds undergraduate and master's degrees in electrical engineering from Stanford University.

Makoto Yano is Chairman of the Research Institute of Economy, Trade and Industry (RIETI); he is also a specially appointed professor at Kyoto University, Jochi University, and Chubu University. He is an internationally known researcher who has made a number of substantial contributions in international trade, market theory, and especially on economic dynamics. His contributions in economic dynamics, for example, are represented by articles in *Econometrica* in 1995 and the *Journal of Economic Theory* in 1996, which explained the conditions under which general economic equilibrium shows chaotic behavior. His 1998 *Econometrica* article is recognized as the latest most important work on the characterization of dynamic general equilibrium.

Besides those rather theoretical works, Prof. Yano has also provided influential insights on contemporary real-world phenomena. Those include transfer problems (*American Economic Review*, 1999), voluntary export restraints (*International Economic Review* [IER], 1995), and trade conflicts (IER, 1998), on which there have been a number of follow-up papers.

His recent research on "market quality" addresses various problems in modern economies, including the financial market crisis since 2008 and the recent nuclear accidents in Japan, from the point of view of market quality—a new economic concept that Prof. Yano has developed and is applying to Japanese and international markets. Concerning quality of competition, quality of information, and quality of products, market quality is defined as an index jointly determined by the efficiency of an allocation and the fairness of the prices that are achieved in a market.

Prof. Yano received a B.A. in economics from The University of Tokyo in 1971 and a Ph.D. in economics from The University of Rochester in 1981.

Chapter 3
Industrial Applications of Blockchain to IoT Data

Steven Pu

1 IoT and Blockchain

1.1 Challenges Facing the IoT Space

Blockchain has been long touted as the perfect technological complement to IoT systems. To understand why there has been such enthusiasm for the synergies between these two seemingly unrelated technology systems, we first examine some of the largest challenges facing the IoT space, divided into several broad categories: technological, commercial, and social.

1.1.1 Technical Challenges

Contemporary IoT systems increasingly exist and interface in a sea of connected devices that are not only potentially adversarial, but also often operate on heterogenous infrastructure and standards. This coupled with the fact that IoT devices are being deployed at an accelerated rate (Columbus 2018) makes these hitherto rather obscure technological concerns increasingly relevant to our daily lives. Here we examine several key technical challenges to IoT systems.

From a network perspective, IoT devices predominantly exist in networks that have a hub-and-spoke topology, or a server–client paradigm. Each connected device can be considered as an endpoint that constantly needs to communicate with a central

This article is based on our final report to the study group "Blockchain and Society 5.0—The Creation of a New Marketplace based on Distributed Consensus" at the Research Institute of Economy, Trade, and Industry (RIETI).

S. Pu (✉)
Taraxa, San Jose, CA, USA
e-mail: steven.pu@taraxa.io

M. Yano et al. (eds.), *Blockchain and Crypto Currency*, Economics, Law, and Institutions in Asia Pacific,
https://doi.org/10.1007/978-981-15-3376-1_3

server to upload data, communicate with other devices, and receive commands. In most networks, even when the IoT devices are just a few feet apart, they cannot communicate with each other directly and must rely upon this centralized server to broker such communication. This centralized server, while it may be a distributed network of computers, is still a centrally administered entity and therefore presents a single point of failure. This means that to compromise (to render inoperable, or to take outright control over) a large network of IoT devices, all the attacker needs to do is to compromise or take control of the central server these devices are reliant upon for everything from sending and receiving commands to data uploads. This presents not just a significant security risk but also an administrative nightmare to those who operate such central IoT management services.

In addition to presenting a single point of failure, centrally managed IoT networks also place the entire upfront investment, ongoing management costs, storage and computation **workload** involved with the management and maintenance on a single entity. As IoT networks become more ubiquitous, interconnected, and scale from hundreds of millions to trillions of devices, this type of centralized workload becomes rapidly untenable. This especially becomes a problem for device **maintenance** as technology advances forward and each centralized network management system needs to keep ever-increasing versions of software and firmware (many of which have become obsolete) and be able to make them available on demand to ensure the longevity of IoT devices that have been deployed in the field.

At the endpoints (often sensors) within the network, most IoT devices still rely upon plaintext passwords and worse, manufacturers' default or commonly reused passwords to establish **identity** and privileges on the network across devices, making them vulnerable to attacks by malware such as Mirai (Graff 2017). Such poor security practices are not only driven by a general lack of security awareness and understanding but also by the complexity that comes with managing such a large and disparate set of connected devices in a central system. These passwords further limit the security of these devices' communications because there is no way beyond communicating with the central server to validate the identity, origin, and, by extension, veracity of the messages (or collected data) as is commonly guaranteed by modern crypto graphical methods.

Without cryptographically guaranteed identities, signatures, and identity-based encryption, data collected by and sent from most IoT devices today cannot establish **provenance** and therefore cannot be trusted unless the data (and any fallout from bad data) is guaranteed by a trusted third party, which greatly increases the communication and more importantly, transactional friction between devices. This presents a further security risk that the unencrypted or poorly encrypted data could have been intercepted or worse, tampered with while in transmission, which further erodes the trust other entities (e.g., other people, companies, devices) have for the resultant data and could potentially damage the reputation of the IoT network's owner.

Looking at IoT as a sector, IoT networks are invariably made up of extremely long value chains comprising many disparate components and players. Using dataflow as a connecting dimension, there are sensors that collect the data at the endpoints, gateways that manage the sensors and aggregate as well as upload the data, storage systems (e.g., cloud) that store and make the data available, and analytics engines that digest and generate actionable insights from the data. Within each step and between these steps, all the hardware and software involved must agree to a set of common **standards** by which to communicate, and those standards are just as disparate as the innumerable number of players in the IoT space. This results in the entire IoT industry being severely siloed, with completely disparate IoT systems that do not and technically cannot communicate, much less transact, with one another. The difficulty in facilitating communications between these siloed and heterogenous networks is one of the biggest technical challenges in IoT today and is holding back the massive network effect potential of the IoT space.

1.1.2 Business Challenges

Despite the many rosy predictions for the future of IoT (Columbus 2018), most businesses still have serious reservations when it comes to making serious investments into IoT and IoT-related systems. Besides the numerous technical challenges, there are serious business challenges such as the generally unclear (or outright lack of) business case, data sensitivity, and the potential strategic risk of sharing data.

Return on investment inevitably drives business decisions, and investment into IoT is no different. One of the biggest challenges for IoT is the lack of a viable **business case** that justifies its investments, either by generating revenue or shaving costs. Business cases are difficult to come by because it is extremely hard to figure out how to analyze and generate value from the data collected by IoT devices.

To fully capture the value of data often requires specialized expertise, an expertise that businesses that generate data generally lack. This lack of internal expertise requires businesses to seek outside help, which often raises concerns for **data sensitivity**, driving businesses to be very careful and highly selective about which partners and vendors they collaborate with to analyze the data. This cautious approach no doubt severely circumscribes the extent to which any business has access to the best possible talent to analyze and generate value from their data sets and greatly reduces the possibility of finding a viable business case. This problem is further exacerbated given that many breakthrough value-generating insights come from data that is aggregated from many businesses and often across industry verticals, but with each business closely guarding their data nest eggs such insights become nearly impossible to discover.

Even when businesses are comfortable sharing data with a specific vendor, there still exists the potentially fatal **strategic risk** that the vendor (usually a technology platform) will overtake the business with superior aggregation of and insights generated from data. As data is increasingly seen as a critical driver of performance, efficiency, and profitability, it has also become a strategic resource. Large technology platforms (e.g., Google, Amazon, Facebook) gain long-term sustainable competitive advantages through effective aggregation and analytics of data and have established de facto monopolistic power. Not only are such platforms able to dominate the technology markets they were born out of, but with their proprietary technology and massive data aggregation and analytics, they have proven consistently capable of disrupting a variety of markets that are not even adjacent to their original core businesses (e.g., Google with automotive, Apple with gaming, Amazon with cloud) . Hence, by aggregating and effectively analyzing data, the "vendor" can then turn back on the "client" and invade its markets.

1.1.3 Social Challenges

With the rapid proliferation of digitized technologies, the public at large has become increasingly aware of the omnipresence of data-collecting sensors as well as concerned about how they are being used. Recent scandals involving Facebook (Granville 2018) and Google's (MacMillan and McMillan 2018) mishandling of user data sparked worldwide concerns amongst the public as well as regulators. The EU's General Data Protection Regulation (GDPR) (EU GDPR.ORG 2018) that came into effect in May of 2018 further placed privacy and data ownership at the center of civil discourse. These regulatory trends, however, are still extremely limited in scope in that they mostly require user consent upon visiting websites that only *acknowledges* the problem without fundamentally solving it. These concerns are especially thorny in the case of IoT devices, because they have increasingly become embedded directly into our environments without our knowledge, tracking everything from location and movement to voice and video. Much of this also happens with numerous third parties whose involvement and activities are difficult to track, as well as across political jurisdictions each with their uniquely different regulatory requirements, further complicating social concerns. If IoT technology is to continue to proliferate, it must address **data privacy** concerns head-on and provide socially acceptable solutions to guarantee secure data ownership and usage without triggering innovation-killing regulatory backlashes.

1.2 Blockchain Empowers IoT Devices

Although the first and most widely known application of blockchains is Bitcoin, its underlying technologies provide a unique suite of functionalities that make it uniquely complementary to IoT by empowering them to become independent entities within a decentralized network. In doing so, this development directly or indirectly addresses many of the challenges currently facing IoT technologies.

1.2.1 Blockchain Grants Devices Independence

IoT devices in today's networks do not exist as independent entities outside of their centrally managed networks. As far as the outside world is concerned, they are dealing with a large server sitting in the cloud that has some data, without any idea of the provenance of the data or any means to interact directly with the devices that collected the data in the first place. On a blockchain network, each node—any participant connected to the network—has a unique private and public key pair that uniquely identifies it as an independent participant on the network. Specifically, these identities are enforced largely using cryptographic signatures, or digital messages that unmistakably (and next to impossible to forge) identify the sender.

Having unique identities is the foundation for achieving independence, giving each device the ability to act on its behalf. This enables a decentralized mesh network topology rather than a centralized server–client network topology, with each node able to make its own decisions, and, more importantly, to make use of its own resources independently of the other nodes. This type of network is much more secure, because hackers can no longer gain control over millions of devices by hacking a single server (a single point of failure). Rather, the hacker has to compromise millions of devices one by one, with each compromised device likely to be rejected by the network for misbehavior, resulting in the hacker taking over a useless, disconnected device.

A decentralized network with a smart consensus algorithm is also much better at balancing workloads that were formerly handled by a single entity. This makes network deployment as well as maintenance far less costly because the workload of connectivity, storage, and even computation can now be done by many devices in the network, without the need for a costly centralized arbiter.

1.2.2 Blockchain Grants Devices Awareness for Ownership

Blockchain also endows devices with the concept of ownership through the very same cryptographic primitives that guaranteed unique identities. Any device can now sign for as well as encrypt any form of digital asset it has access to. Specifically, a device can now own cryptocurrencies (like Bitcoin) as well as other forms of assets that it has control over (e.g., data, bandwidth, storage). By having this concept of ownership, the IoT device is now an independent economic entity able to not only act, but act in its own best economic interests. For example, instead of remaining idle, a device might decide to put its capabilities on auction and collect customized data on-demand; to avoid obsolescence, it could network with other similar devices to contract order a firmware upgrade, etc. While they like science fiction, these examples may not be too far off in the future.

Guaranteeing ownership of digitized assets also guarantees the privacy of the asset generator. Without the explicit permission of the originator, e.g., without a decryption key, no one can access the data. Today's rampant, and, more importantly, hidden data collection and aggregation processes will be brought to the forefront and forced to seek explicit permission from the data generator and owner.

1.2.3 Blockchain Enables Devices to Trade

What does an independent, asset-owning economic entity do? It trades with other independent, asset-owning entities. At the core of every blockchain network is a consensus algorithm that makes sure every node on the network agrees on the network's historical set of state transitions, or, more simply, what has changed about the network. This consensus enables the defining functionality of blockchain—decentralized trading of digitized assets.

The ability to securely trade assets and resources becomes even more consequential when you consider the global ecosystem of open-source developers that are naturally part of any open-source blockchain ecosystem. Now there is a way to reward and enable better usage of the data collected by devices in a decentralized manner. Any device or a network of devices can choose to publish a segment of its collected data and put up a bounty with a specific objective (e.g., lower energy consumption, faster processing throughput) on the blockchain marketplace, locking the reward in a cryptographically guaranteed smart contract, and incentivize people (and intelligent algorithms) to discover and be rewarded for the solution. Discovering uses (business models) for data was an extremely difficult problem for a centralized entity, but with blockchain, it could potentially become a much simpler decentralized problem, tapping into a globalized talent pool from all over the world.

1.3 Current Limitations to the IoT + Blockchain Vision

With blockchain technology, IoT devices are empowered to make independent decisions, work together to distribute workload and maintenance, and freely trade assets and resources with localized decision-making. Continuation down this path will see the development of an intelligent, self-evolving, self-governing network that we have seen described only in science fiction.

Although the advent of blockchain technology means that we are many steps closer to this futuristic vision, we are not quite there yet. Some of the key limitations of the system are listed below.

- There lacks a mainstream, demonstrable low-latency, high-throughput blockchain network designed specifically for IoT devices.
- Device manufacturers have yet to embed cryptographic keys into every piece of hardware or make them blockchain-compatible as a generalized standard.
- Software cryptographic methods to guaranteeing privacy-preserving computations are grossly inefficient and not practical (IBM Research Editorial Staff 2018), while hardware solutions require trust in the manufacturer and the entire manufacturing supply chain, making it difficult to protect against data piracy.
- Artificial intelligence is not sufficiently sophisticated to enable such extraordinarily autonomous decision-making behavior in devices.

- Legal recourse is still required to further de-risk trading over blockchain, but only limited jurisdictions (De 2018) have recognized smart contracts on blockchain as legally binding contracts off-chain.

In time, however, we are optimistic that all the above-mentioned limitations will be overcome.

Even with these limitations, blockchain is still well positioned to resolve many of the technological, business, and social challenges faced by IoT with wide-ranging potential for value-adding applications. We now dive deeper into the current state of blockchain technology to see what else can be done to improve upon the state of the art.

2 A Blockchain Network Created for IoT Devices

Given all the synergies between blockchain and IoT, what are the characteristics of a blockchain network that would be well suited for IoT needs? Although much blockchain technology is infrastructural in nature and is not obviously application specific, there are many design and optimization choices in the public ledger level that should reflect what application stacks the designers were thinking about during the development process.

2.1 Characteristics IoT Devices and Implications on the Design of Blockchain Networks

When thinking about IoT, specifically in contrast with the nodes that operate on existing blockchain networks, it is useful to know that all blockchain networks today rely on the services of powerful and constantly connected servers to perform all the record-keeping and consensus duties. What is immediately apparent is that most of what we think of as "IoT" devices, or smaller, sometimes mobile, connected devices, have limited and unique characteristics that do not fit this profile.

While the term "IoT" is used to refer basically to any connected device, we could make several general statements about the characteristics of these devices.

- **Massive scale**: by some estimates (Tung 2017) the number of IoT devices has already surpassed the human population in the world, and will continue to grow at an accelerated rate.
- **Limited computing power**: IoT devices are usually not processing powerhouses often by orders of magnitude even compared to the processing power in regular laptop computers (TrueBench 2018).
- **Limited storage**: most IoT devices are not meant to store information locally and are simply meant to relay information (e.g., to a cloud), hence have very limited storage.

- **Limited bandwidth and connectivity**: many IoT devices operate out in the field without reliable connections and costly connectivity (e.g., satellite network in the middle of the woods).
- **Limited power consumption**: many IoT devices operate on batteries or via energy-harvesting mechanisms that place severe constraints on its energy consumption.

The design challenge can then be formulated thus: what are the critical metrics required to design a blockchain network that can best serve IoT devices?

1. **Network needs to be scalable**: given there could be potentially billions of devices connected to any given blockchain network, the network must be able to scale its capacity in processing transactions and requests.
2. **Network needs to support discovery and trading of generic digital assets**: IoT devices have many digital assets and resources (e.g., data) to trade, not simply currency, and they need means of discovering these assets.
3. **Network needs to support selective memory**: given all the limitations of IoT devices, they will only be able to participate in a small subset of the network and must be selective in what each device stores and processes.
4. **Network cannot solely depend on "work" to maintain security**: network security cannot be purely based on solving complex cryptographic puzzles, making blockchain transactions impractical for IoT devices.
5. **Network needs to support trustless light nodes**: IoT devices today cannot support full node operations but still need to maintain their independence on a blockchain network. The "light" nodes run on IoT devices therefore cannot be naïve (i.e., blindly trusting another full node) and must have some means of validating network state and state transitions.
6. **Network needs to support point-to-point transactions**: many transactions between IoT devices are highly localized—the devices are right next to each other—and cannot be expected to wait for the latency of network-wide validation every time.

With these design goals in mind, the Taraxa project was started to help IoT devices democratize their data and maximize the value generated by that data.

2.2 An Evolving Landscape

When Taraxa was first being conceived in 2017, significant research was conducted into the existing slate of blockchain networks as well as relevant technologies to understand not just the current landscape but also how the space has evolved over time. While there are many amazing projects doing important work and making major contributions to the blockchain space, we acknowledge a few projects that not only inspired but made possible in many ways our work here at Taraxa.

2.2.1 Bitcoin

As of this writing, it has been exactly 10 years (Investopedia 2018) since the first publication of Satoshi Nakamoto's whitepaper (Nakamoto 2008) and the beginning of the blockchain revolution. While all the technologies underlying Bitcoin were not new and in fact similar incarnations had been proposed and even implemented before (Narayanan and Clark 2017), Bitcoin was unique in that its designs not only incorporated these technologies in an innovative way, but also built in the ideas of decentralization, trustless transactions, and a sophisticated understanding of human incentives.

Probably most consequentially, Bitcoin's arrival coincided with a global crisis of trust as the world was descending into one of the worst financial crises in recorded history (Bernanke 2018). Ordinary citizens worldwide were questioning not only the seemingly absolute authority that centralized entities such as the global banking system and large multinational corporations have over everyone's daily lives, but also the implicit trust that is placed in these institutions. Bitcoin is unique for being the very first representation of *value outside the system* (a term coined by investor and blockchain entrepreneur Jianbo Wang) of existing institutions' underwriting, approval, or participation.

Bitcoin is the technological and philosophical inspiration for the entire blockchain space.

2.2.2 Ethereum

By expanding beyond (or rather completely rewriting) Bitcoin's simple scripting language into a Turing complete application layer called smart contracts, Ethereum (Ethereum White Paper 2018) has enabled potentially an infinite number of applications to take advantage of blockchain's unique properties beyond simply currency.

Ethereum made possible many decentralized applications, including games, marketplaces, and even decentralized corporations. The explosion of applications drew interest and participation from far beyond just the financial sector, but also from many mainstream academic, industrial, and public institutions. Along with Ethereum also arose the initial coin offerings, a fundraising model that offers the first viable alternative to the existing and highly centralized global investment apparatus, giving many nascent decentralized projects a chance to grow.

Ethereum is what sparked our imagination that blockchain could be much more than just a currency.

2.2.3 IOTA

IOTA (Popov 2018) was the first widely known project (many lesser-known projects proposed similar technologies during roughly the same time period) to propose an alternative data structure (a directed acyclic graph, or DAG) as opposed to the typical blockchain pioneered by Bitcoin. It was also the first project to educate the wider market of the synergies between IoT and blockchain. Although at times controversial (Narula 2017), IOTA nevertheless has made and continues to make important contributions to the blockchain space.

2.2.4 ByteBall

ByteBall (Churyumov 2016) was the first widely known project to propose total ordering within a DAG blockchain network by identifying a main chain as a set of anchors. Via this main chain, every node would run a deterministic algorithm that eventually converges onto the same total-network ordering with minimal communication overhead. This mainchain resolves the convergent ordering issue for DAG networks while making use of every vertex (in the case of Byteball, they are transactions) on the DAG.

2.2.5 Phantom

Proposed by authors of the influential papers Ghost (Sompolinsky and Zohar 2013) and Spectre (Sompolinsky et al. 2016), Phantom (Sompolinsky and Zohar 2018) is a blockchain that proposes the blockDAG, a way to organize sets of transactions like those in Bitcoin and Ethereum blocks into a DAG topology, and then converges upon a single chain via a deterministic algorithm that each node executes individually. The blockDAG combined many of the concurrent properties of a DAG while also maintaining the idea of a transaction set, enabling many of Taraxa's innovations in concurrency.

2.3 *Taraxa's Innovations*

Every blockchain infrastructure project should seek to introduce technical innovations to the blockchain space and contribute to the cumulative pool of open-source knowledge, and Taraxa is no different. Building on the existing body of knowledge and technologies, we set out to make the following key contributions as roughly summarized below.

2.3.1 Concurrent Smart Contracts

As it stands today, smart contracts are processed in sequential order by nodes on blockchain networks. Taraxa implements a way to process them concurrently (i.e., in parallel) to increase the processing throughput of smart contracts.

There are several obstacles to running smart contracts in parallel. First, because smart contracts modify shared storage (their persistent storage), it is crucial to keep track of which processes are accessing which areas of storage at any given moment to avoid conflicting access. Second, because the programming language is Turing complete, it is impossible to determine statically whether different contract calls will conflict during parallel execution.

We propose that the Taraxa nodes execute smart contract code as speculative actions. A node schedules multiple smart contract calls for parallel execution, and then keeps track of their access to persistent storage via the Taraxa runtime APIs. Should there be conflicting access (i.e., read/write, write/write), the access is rejected, the conflict is reported to the scheduler, with the scheduler terminating the process, rolling back its speculative changes to the persistent storage, and reschedules these conflicting contract calls for sequential processing.

We further propose that to minimize the number of conflicts during execution, we endow the virtual machine with partial semantic understanding for the code. In general, a computer simply executes code it is given without the need or capability to understand what it is actually doing; that is, the code has no meaning (semantics) to the machine. However, many types of executions may look like conflicts but are in fact not true conflicts if the computer understands their purpose. For example, many contracts make use of counters to enforce a specific range; hence, the order of operations (i.e., increments, decrements) on this counter is not important, because the result remains the same no matter the order they occur, as long as they do not exceed the range. Hence, what may look like conflicts with multiple calls accessing the same counter is in fact not necessarily a conflict. The virtual machine may be endowed with such semantic understanding through analysis of the byte code and automatically tagging operations that fit a specific pattern; for example, a counter.

In addition to executions, we also propose that the process of committing (writing) state transitions into persistent storage could also be parallelized.

Note that all concurrency gains are obtained without the developers needing to alter their coding behavior or their code. This is especially important because any new technology that involves more work on the part of the developers is less likely to be adopted.

With contracts now processed in parallel, it is important for other nodes to follow the same concurrent schedule, or else every node will select a different set of contract calls with different concurrent schedules and there is no convergent consensus. Hence, a concurrent schedule will be embedded along with the concurrent set to ensure that all nodes execute the concurrent set in the exact same order as agreed upon (via consensus) and arrive at the same resultant state.

2.3.2 Fuzzy Sharding

To take full advantage of multiple nodes working together to make progress on the network, Taraxa makes use of a blockDAG topology, pioneered by researchers of the Phantom (Sompolinsky and Zohar 2018) paper. This topology has the advantage of enabling multiple nodes to work together to propose blocks and help the network make progress, but it then potentially suffers from nodes simultaneously performing redundant work.

Taraxa proposes a set of algorithms that elegantly resolves these issues without coordination. In most other networks, the functionality of which nodes are responsible for which separate tasks require the election of a leader, who has temporary power over a certain set of decisions, such as which node is assigned which work. The election of a leader is expensive in terms of network resources and exposes that specific leader to attacks once its identity is known. Using a set of cryptographic operations (cryptographic sortition), Taraxa allows each node to independently verify proposal eligibility and transaction jurisdiction—in other words, they are assigned non-overlapping tasks, randomly and fairly, without the need for a leader to coordinate them.

Trustless Light Nodes

While IoT devices lack the resources necessary to host a "full node," that does not mean they cannot retain their independence or contribute to core ledger tasks. Taraxa creates a series of light node designs that can accommodate the full spectrum of IoT devices, from the most resource-starved to those that are less so. Indeed, the term "full node" is one extreme on a spectrum, referring to powerful computers with significant computation, storage, bandwidth resource, and high uptime, while the term "light node" refers to the remaining spectrum of devices that do not fit this profile. Any light node design must accommodate the spectrum, giving each device the choice to participate as much or as little as it is capable. Any network that constrains proper execution of its protocol to only those devices with a high threshold of computing power is inherently creating a centralizing force. In addition, keeping the bar low for device participation means that more powerful nodes present an attack vector, and more generally represent wasted computing effort. Therefore, given the twin desires to both maximize decentralization and performance, the protocol must enable this wide spectrum of devices to participate to their fullest.

In Taraxa's designs, light nodes will be able to be more trustless, in that they are better able to validate the information they receive from the network. In conventional designs, light nodes simply latch onto a specific full node and request an update, while only able to validate the internal consistency of what it has been told (e.g., there is no contradictory information). Taraxa allows a light node to randomly sample a subset of the network's full nodes to compare their responses to become more trustless in its validation process.

In addition to validation, light nodes could be made even more trustless by gaining the ability to propose concurrent sets. Given the blockDAG topology, we could enable an efficient merging of concurrent sets proposed by active nodes on the network, allowing for smaller sets to be proposed and still be useful. While light nodes cannot propose arbitrarily large concurrent sets, a sufficiently well-connected node with reasonable storage could propose concurrent sets pertaining to accounts it has on store, perhaps including not just its own account states but also those entities the device regularly interacts with. By enabling light nodes to propose concurrent sets, we also move away from reliance upon powerful computers to maintain the blockchain network (as all existing blockchain projects do) and into the edge with the IoT devices themselves.

Lastly, instead of relying upon solving cryptographic puzzles (i.e., proof-of-work; PoW) to deter spamming attacks, Taraxa will rely on a system of fees, because most IoT devices are unable to complete such puzzles in timely fashion and simplifying such puzzles would render them a useless deterrent to more powerful machines. PoW is just another form of fees that requires upfront capital outlay for better hardware, an option unavailable to most IoT devices.

These are some of what we consider to be Taraxa's primary innovative contributions that could help IoT devices to transact more freely and simply with each other and the world at large.

3 Potential Applications

3.1 Blockchain Application Suitability

Here we briefly outline a few key characteristics of blockchain technology that help to guide what blockchain should and should not be used for. For the purposes of this chapter, blockchain refers to purely public ledgers.

3.1.1 Blockchain Bridges Trust Gaps

Blockchain is a decentralized and distributed network. Being distributed means there are redundant copies of ownership and transactional history so it is difficult to attack the network, while being decentralized means that no participant needs to trust any other participant because agreement is reached through consensus and cryptographic algorithms. Not only is this guaranteed during transactions; blockchain's unique interlocking data structure enables trivial ex post facto auditing, making data tampering immediately obvious.

By bridging trust gaps, blockchain enables formerly impossible or grossly inefficient market-making, and simplification or entire removal of inefficient trust-building apparatus within existing markets.

3.1.2 Blockchain Is Digital

Although the digital nature of blockchain may sound obvious, blockchain technologies are only applicable when dealing with digital assets. The first application of blockchain was Bitcoin, a digital currency (a form of digital asset) encoded as balances and transfers that are wholly self-contained within the blockchain. Other digital assets might represent data created off-chain and then anchored and traded on-chain (e.g., IoT data, digital content), or are digital representations of physical assets (e.g., asset-backed securities).

3.1.3 Blockchain's Guarantees Are on-Chain Only

While blockchain provides many security and trustless guarantees on-chain, it is important to note that all such guarantees are *only* on-chain. Should parties make off-chain arrangements that erode the integrity of on-chain transactions (e.g., collusion between Bitcoin miners), there is little that the blockchain can do about it. Robust blockchain design can seek to minimize or thwart bribery in critical consensus and validation steps, but it cannot solve the fundamental problem that potential off-chain value may be greater than the value proposition of honest on-chain behavior. In contrast, when on-chain, blockchain protocols are designed to tolerate a fair proportion of "dishonest" nodes (up to 30% or even up to 50% of the network) without fundamental loss of network integrity.

3.1.4 Blockchain Is Inefficient

Blockchain's trustless transactions come at the cost of efficiency. Having to constantly reach consensus and replicate transactions across the network, possibly in the presence of faulty, confused, and dishonest nodes, makes blockchain networks fundamentally inefficient. This means blockchain should be used sparingly when security and trust concerns outweigh the benefits of efficiency.

Above all, blockchain should be leveraged as a way to keep centralized systems honest. Centralized systems have clear performance advantages over decentralized systems such as blockchain and are required for any performance-sensitive applications. There is no reason to want only replace centralized systems with decentralized systems.

3.2 Potential IoT Applications by Archetype

At Taraxa, we identified three distinct categories of IoT-relevant blockchain applications. Because this is a nascent and rapidly evolving space, this only represents our latest thinking at the time of writing.

3.2.1 IoT Data Anchoring

IoT devices generate a great deal of data, and when that data is shared across entities it needs to be trusted. One way to augment trust is to establish unique identities for each data-generating device and have the devices anchor the data they have collected onto the blockchain.

The anchoring process involves placing a hash (a function that maps data of arbitrary size into data of fixed size in a way that minimizes collisions—different pieces of data cannot map into the same hash) of a data set collected by the device along with its signature into say a smart contract as a record of the provenance of the data as well as proof that the data has not been tampered with. Only the hash of the data set should be stored on-chain, and not the full data set, because we want to minimize the load and cost of using the blockchain, and the signature guarantees that the data came from the device. Of course, this would also require that the device manufacturer publish the public keys embedded (preferably via secure hardware) into their devices.

Examples:

- **Cold chain logistics**: a supermarket that is taking delivery of milk shipped via cold chain would like to have guarantees that the milk has been properly refrigerated throughout its route. If the refrigeration units were turned off during shipping for a few hours and turned back on, the supermarket would not be able to tell the difference until the milk started to spoil much earlier than expected. Location and temperature sensors could be installed on each refrigerated truck. These would intermittently upload data as well as anchor that data onto the blockchain, ensuring that the shipping company has not tampered with the data after the event.
- **Public infrastructure monitoring**: with the advent of public–private partnerships, many local governments are increasingly outsourcing the management and maintenance of public infrastructure such as bridges, roads, and tunnels to private companies. Once outsourced, the government has a responsibility to ensure that public infrastructure is being well maintained and that the data reported are accurate (e.g., toll income, maintenance expenditure). Sensors installed on such public infrastructure (e.g., cameras, strain gauges, moisture) will also anchor the data they collect onto the blockchain to prove to local governments that the data has not been tampered with.

3.2.2 Machine Monetization and Eventual Tokenization

Many assets being monitored by sensors are revenue-generating machines that require significant upfront capital outlay to deploy. For many new ventures, obtaining funding or loans through traditional financing channels may be challenging.

With proper data anchoring, the earning capabilities of such machines can be tracked in real time on the blockchain, providing proof and generating expectations for future income. Businesses can then solicit potential customers to invest in shares of these machines by issuing digital tokens on the blockchain. This has the dual benefit of not only raising funds from a much wider pool of potential investors, but also that the tokens are likely to end up in the hands of customers who have interest in purchasing the services of the machine in the future.

Examples:

- **Shared vehicles**: require the operator to not only make large upfront investments to purchase a fleet of cars but also run continuous and aggressive marketing campaigns to generate awareness. If each vehicle's location, movement, mileage, and, most importantly, income data were to be released to the public (anonymized to protect driver privacy), each vehicle could be tokenized and those who purchase the tokens would receive a heavy discount when renting the shared vehicle. Not only does this alleviate the pressure of extremely large upfront investments, it also ties customers into an ecosystem that they now have a stake in and financial incentives into drive the service's adoption, elegantly killing two birds with one stone.
- **Smart vending machines**: vending machines are becoming increasingly popular around the world as a low-cost and highly convenient alternative to manned storefronts, but their value remains underutilized. With so many machines deployed on every street corner, they could easily be outfitted with additional IoT infrastructure to enable them to collect data of their surroundings (e.g., foot and vehicle traffic, localized weather) which could be sold, become distribution points for humanitarian aid (e.g., disaster relief, charitable giving), or even serve up a far more accurate alternative geo-location service (e.g., via WiFi triangulation) in an urban environment to GPS. All of which could not only help further monetize these vending machines but also provide social services far beyond their original design goals.

Machine to Machine Economy

The ultimate application is to enable machines to trade with one another autonomously. This of course would require a very high level of intelligence and autonomy on the part of the machines, but a variety of mechanisms could be designed where machines can discover and purchase resources they require to optimally complete their stated objectives.

One of the most common mechanisms is a marketplace; here we look at two potential applications.

- **Agricultural drones** could make real-time decisions on plant protection (e.g., insecticide) deployment across a field based on its internal models and by purchasing data from the surrounding sensors. It could purchase or trade data with cameras in the surrounding fields for analytics on pest detection, from local weather sensors to predict chances of rain so that the chemicals will not be washed off minutes after deployment, from local soil moisture sensors to customize the level of dilution, etc. Once machines are automated by AI and empowered by blockchain, they can operate and interact with one another with minimal intervention.

- **Traffic routing** for autonomous vehicles may be very different than for vehicles operated by humans. Vehicles could, in real time, communicate their intended destination, urgency, and willingness to pay surrounding vehicles so that traffic could be routed and reshaped in real time according to supply and demand. Usual visual and audio cues created for human drivers would not be necessary (e.g., traffic lights, turn signals), and in their place would be a dynamic real time bidding market for road space as a commodity.

References

Bernanke BS (2018) The real effects of the financial crisis. In: BPEA conference draft, vol Fall

Churyumov A (2016) Byteball: a decentralized system for storage and transfer of value, 1 Oct 2016 [Online]. Available: https://byteball.org/Byteball.pdf. Accessed 17 Dec 2018

Columbus L (2018) 10 charts that will challenge your perspective of IoT's growth. Forbes, 6 June 2018 [Online]. Available: https://www.forbes.com/sites/louiscolumbus/2018/06/06/10-charts-that-will-challenge-your-perspective-of-iots-growth/#47c74fd13ecc. Accessed 15 Nov 2018

De N (2018) Smart contracts now recognized under Tennessee Law. Coindesk, 23 Mar 2018 [Online]. Available: https://www.coindesk.com/blockchain-bill-becomes-law-tennessee. Accessed 15 Nov 2018

Ethereum White Paper (2018) 21 Aug 2018 [Online]. Available: https://github.com/ethereum/wiki/wiki/White-Paper. Accessed 17 Dec 2018

EU GDPR.ORG (2018) GDPR FAQs. EU GDPR.ORG [Online]. Available: https://eugdpr.org/the-regulation/gdpr-faqs/. Accessed 15 Nov 2018

Graff GM (2017) How a dorm room minecraft scam brought down the internet. WIRED, 13 Dec 2017 [Online]. Available: https://www.wired.com/story/mirai-botnet-minecraft-scam-brought-down-the-internet/. Accessed 15 Nov 2018

Granville K (2018) Facebook and Cambridge analytica: what you need to know as fallout widens. The New York Times, 19 Mar 2018 [Online]. Available: https://www.nytimes.com/2018/03/19/technology/facebook-cambridge-analytica-explained.html. Accessed 15 Nov 2018

IBM Research Editorial Staff (2018) Elegant, disgusting cryptography. IBM, 21 Mar 2018 [Online]. Available: https://www.ibm.com/blogs/research/2018/03/elegant-disgusting-cryptography/. Accessed 15 Nov 2018

Investopedia (2018) Bitcoin. Investopedia [Online]. Available: https://www.investopedia.com/terms/b/bitcoin.asp. Accessed 31 Oct 2018

MacMillan D, McMillan R (2018) Google exposed user data, feared repercussions of disclosing to public. Wall Street Journal, 8 Oct 2018 [Online]. Available: https://www.wsj.com/articles/google-exposed-user-data-feared-repercussions-of-disclosing-to-public-1539017194. Accessed 15 Nov 2018

Nakamoto S (2008) Bitcoin: a peer-to-peer electronic cash system, 31 Oct 2008 [Online]. Available: https://bitcoin.org/bitcoin.pdf. Accessed 31 Oct 2018

Narayanan A, Clark J (2017) Bitcoin's academic pedigree. acmqueue 15(4)

Narula N (2017) Cryptographic vulnerabilities in IOTA. Medium, 7 Sept 2017 [Online]. Available: https://medium.com/@neha/cryptographic-vulnerabilities-in-iota-9a6a9ddc4367. Accessed 2 Nov 2018

Popov S (2018) The tangle, 30 Apr 2018 [Online]. Available: https://assets.ctfassets.net/r1dr6vzfxhev/2t4uxvsIqk0EUau6g2sw0g/45eae33637ca92f85dd9f4a3a218e1ec/iota1_4_3.pdf. Accessed 17 Dec 2018

Sompolinsky Y, Zohar A (2013) Secure high-rate transaction processing in bitcoin. 2013 [Online]. Available: https://eprint.iacr.org/2013/881.pdf. Accessed 17 Dec 2018

Sompolinsky Y, Lewenberg Y, Zohar A (2016) SPECTRE: serialization of proof-of-work events: confirming transactions via recursive elections, 2016 [Online]. Available: https://eprint.iacr.org/2016/1159.pdf. Accessed 17 Dec 2018

Sompolinsky Y, Zohar A (2018) PHANTOM, GHOSTDAG: two scalable blockDAG protocols. 2018 [Online]. Available: https://eprint.iacr.org/2018/104.pdf. Accessed 17 Dec 2018

Tung L (2017) IoT devices will outnumber the world's population this year for the first time. ZDNet, 7 Feb 2017 [Online]. Available: https://www.zdnet.com/article/iot-devices-will-outnumber-the-worlds-population-this-year-for-the-first-time/. Accessed 31 Oct 2018

TrueBench (2018) TrueBench, 31 Oct 2018 [Online]. Available: http://truebench.the-toffee-project.org/

World Economic Forum (2018) Blockchain beyond the hype, World Economic Forum, Geneva

Steven Pu is an entrepreneur and strategy consultant. Prior to founding Taraxa, he co-founded multiple venture-funded startups in wireless mesh networks, mobile health, and healthcare services. He was also a director at Monitor Deloitte's China office, spearheading the firm's digital strategy practice, advising senior executives of multinational corporations on how large organizations could effectively capture innovation and respond quickly to market disruptions.

Mr. Pu holds undergraduate and master's degrees in electrical engineering from Stanford University.

Chapter 4
Theory of Money: From Ancient Japanese Copper Coins to Virtual Currencies

Makoto Yano

Currently, virtual currencies are targets of speculative activities and subject to many other problems. If, however, an ideal virtual currency can be realized, it is expected that it will add a whole new dimension to our economic activities.

Virtual currency is very similar to deposit currency in that data is used as money. While deposit currencies are centrally controlled by banks and other financial institutions, virtual currencies are maintained in a decentralized manner by many people. Through decentralization, significant cost savings can be realized.

To evaluate the potential of virtual currencies, it is necessary to understand what a currency is as opposed to money, what divides banknotes from deposit currency, and what separates virtual currency from deposit currency. This chapter covers these issues by introducing a new theory of money.

1 History of Money: From Commodity Money to Virtual Currency

To understand the innovations that virtual currencies have brought, and are expected to bring to our society, it is desirable to study various types of currencies that were

This article is based on my final report to the study group "Blockchain and Society 5.0—The Creation of a New Marketplace based on Distributed Consensus" at the Research Institute of Economy, Trade, and Industry (RIETI) . I am grateful to all the participant in the study group and also to Fumio Dei and William Metcalfe for valuable comments on earlier versions of this chapter. The author gratefully acknowledges the financial support of a Grant-in-Aid for Scientific Research (A) (#16H02015) from the Japan Society for the Promotion of Science.

M. Yano (✉)
Research Institute of Economy, Trade and Industry (RIETI), Tokyo, Japan
e-mail: yano-makoto@rieti.go.jp

M. Yano et al. (eds.), *Blockchain and Crypto Currency*,
Economics, Law, and Institutions in Asia Pacific,
https://doi.org/10.1007/978-981-15-3376-1_4

used in the past and that are used currently, and compare them with virtual currencies. For this purpose, it is useful to start with the history of Japanese money.

1.1 History of Japanese Money

In Japan, twelve kinds of copper coins (called the imperial coins) were cast over the period between 708 AD and 963 AD.[1] After that, however, government-made money was not cast again until the era of Toyotomi Hideyoshi (1537–1598) who, in the 1580s, united Japan after a century-long period of war.

This is partly because most Japanese copper was not suitable for coins because it contained too much sulfur.[2] Instead, Chinese copper coins were imported from China between the middle of the twelfth century through to the fifteenth century. Kiyomori Taira (1118–1181) and Yoshimitsu Ashikaga (1358–1408) led trade with the Song Dynasty (960–1279) and the Ming Dynasty (1368–1644), respectively. A main target of trade was Chinese copper coins. It is known that in the fifteenth century, copper coins circulated rather widely; tolls for bridges and fees for inns were paid in copper coins.[3]

Hideyoshi Toyotomi cast the famous first Japanese gold coin, called Tensho Oban, in 1588.[4] Soon after his death, Iyeyasu Tokugawa (1543–1616) took power in 1600 and cast new gold coins called Keicho Oban and Koban. During the Tokugawa era, various coins were cast and circulated widely.

The first paper money was printed in 1610, which promised payback in silver coins. Subsequently, many local governments printed paper money that promised payback in gold and silver coins.[5]

1.2 Paper Money

The modern economy is built on paper money. The era of paper money can be divided into two subperiods. The first subperiod was that in which paper money was convertible into gold whereas the second period is that of nonconvertible money. To understand how the two types of money have developed, it is useful to look into the history of American money.

[1] *Wadokaichin* in 708, is said to be the first Japanese copper coin that was minted for circulation as a medium of exchange. It is known that several earlier coins were minted although they were considered to be not for circulation; e.g., see Takizawa (1996, Chap. 1) and Takagi (2016, p. 10).

[2] See Mikami (1996, p. 6).

[3] See Mikami (1996, p. 9).

[4] Prior to Tesho Oban, some gold and silver coins were minted in the first half of the sixteenth century. However, they were not for circulation but for gifts. During the latter half of the sixteenth century, gold bullion was used for transactions. For details, see Takagi (2016, p. 66).

[5] See Takizawa (1996, p. 253) and Takagi (2016, p. 113).

1.2.1 Gold Standard

Until the mid-1930s, in the United States, the government guaranteed the conversion of dollar bills for gold, which is called the convertible currency system. Immediately after independence, under the 1792 Coinage Act, the $10 coin was legally defined to contain 16.04 grams of pure gold (in other words, 1 troy ounce of gold = $19.319). Subsequently, the amount of gold was reduced to 15.05 grams under the Coinage Act of 1837 (1 troy ounce of gold = $20.67). Then, in 1900, the Gold Standard Act was passed that set gold as the only standard for redeeming paper money. This conversion rate was kept until 1933.

In the middle of the nineteenth century, there were times when state governments, cities, commercial banks, and various companies issued dollar bills that were convertible for gold and government bonds. Under such a system, once a bank got into financial trouble, many people demanded withdrawal of deposits at once. Such a bank would be doomed to fail because no bank could satisfy a massive demand for withdrawal. That triggered withdrawal demands for other banks which stalled the monetary system as a whole. This phenomenon is called a "bank run."

To deal with this problem, the USA adopted the Federal Reserve Act of 1913. Under this act, the Federal Reserve Bank was designated as the bank for issuing money called Federal Reserve Notes. Federal Reserve Notes gradually replaced various banknotes issued by the government and commercial banks. During this time, consistently, 1 troy ounce of gold was fixed at $20.67.

The collapse of the New York Stock Exchange in 1929 triggered a number of corporate bankruptcies and 744 banks failed in the first 10 months alone. After that, the crisis prolonged, and the economic stagnation continued until 1945, when World War II ended. This is the period called the Great Depression.

In 1932, the Pecora Committee, led by Ferdinand Pecora, was created in the Senate to investigate the causes of the Great Depression. Through the Commission's investigation, it was revealed that during the Great Depression, various shady transactions were conducted. One of the major causes of the Great Depression is that book operations such as reassignment of losses were conducted between banks and their securities subsidiaries and between securities firms and their banking subsidiaries.

1.2.2 Fiat Money System

In the first half of the 1930s, various institutional reforms of the financial market took place to cope with the Great Depression. Of particular importance were the following:

1. Abolishment of the gold standard
2. Creation of the Federal Deposit Insurance Corporation
3. Separation of securities companies and commercial banks
4. Introduction of the information disclosure system to the stock market.

These reforms were to ensure the stability of the banking system and to increase the transparency of the financial market as a whole. Nowadays, all developed countries have adopted much the same financial system. In what follows, the first three reforms are explained, and these are directly related to the monetary system based on fiat money.

Abolishment of the Gold Standard: A decline of a country's economic health makes it difficult for the country to maintain the gold standard. In the USA in 1934, most private possession of gold was outlawed by the Gold Reserve Act of 1934; all individuals who owned gold were required to sell it to the Department of Treasury. The Act devalued the dollar against gold, changing $20.67 per troy ounce to $35.

Creation of the Federal Deposit Insurance Corporation: Once a bank run occurs, as discussed above, it becomes highly difficult for the bank to hold enough cash to cover all demands for withdrawals. If banks can insure against such a risk, the banking system will become more stable. With such a consideration, in 1933, the Federal Deposit Insurance Corporation (FDIC) was established. For the banks that were members of the FDIC, a certain amount of a customer's deposit was covered by insurance in the case of a bank failure.

Separation of securities companies and commercial banks: The Glass–Steagall Act was established in 1933, separating the operations of securities companies and commercial banks. Securities can be thought of as certificates that the issuer promises to pay for future earnings. Selling securities implies that the purpose is to invest in the issuer's business. A securities company is an intermediary that facilitates issuances and resellings of securities. Commercial banks provide settlement mediation services to facilitate payments between account holders. Under the Glass–Steagall Act, commercial banks are dedicated to settlement mediation, and securities firms are concentrated on investment mediation.

1.3 Ledger Currencies

Nowadays, records on bank accounts are kept in the form of digital data. As bank deposits show, payment records on bank account can play the role of a currency, which is called a deposit currency. Virtual currencies on the blockchain are also records of transactions in the form of digital data. As this shows, digital transaction data can be used as a currency if the records are accurate and cannot be tampered with.

A ledger is a "book of permanent record." It is safe to assume that "permanent" in this definition implies both "accurate" and "unfalsifiable." Because both deposit and virtual currencies are kept in the form of a ledger, they may be called ledger currencies.

1.3.1 Deposit Currency: Centralized Data Currency

The most familiar examples of deposit currencies are checking accounts in the USA. Instead of writing a check, nowadays, many people use electronic fund transfers by which money can be transferred online at a very low cost. Deposit currencies started changing our daily life in the late 1970s to the early 1980s. During that period, salaries started to be directly deposited into workers' accounts, whereas before that, people were paid in checks and cash.

Theoretically, a bank can offer a deposit currency to its customers by keeping track of all transactions from one account to another and making sure that a payment from an account at a particular point in time does not exceed the balance at that point in time. The transactions are lined up according to time. Once that record is built, it is easy to extract transactions that are related to a particular account.

Cash is an IOU that stipulates the society owe the holder of cash the purchasing power equal to the value of the IOU. A deposit in a bank account is the bank's IOU to the account holder. It is therefore no wonder that a bank deposit serves as a currency to the extent to which the bank's IOU is trusted by account holders.

Currently, deposit currencies are purely supplementary to paper money. In other words, the system of bank deposit accounts functions as money because customers trust banks to pay cash back whenever they demand withdrawals.

1.3.2 Virtual Currency: Decentralized Ledger Currency

Virtual currency is a new type of ledger currency in which trust is ensured by a mechanism completely different from deposit currency. Deposit currency, which is a traditional ledger currency, is managed centrally by the bank. Many workers' efforts are put into maintaining the integrity of transaction records, which creates trust in those records. Virtual currency, in contrast, maintains the integrity of data by a computer algorithm that involves many people in a decentralized manner creating transaction records. The integrity of the data is maintained neither by a single institution nor a single individual but an algorithm itself together with the many people who independently process data through the algorithm.

What is difficult on the Internet is how to link one account with another, how to keep payment/receipt records between accounts, how to ensure accuracy, and how to create a ledger that will never be tampered with. Blockchain technology, on which many virtual currencies are based, is the first technology to show that these difficulties can be overcome on the Internet in a completely open and decentralized manner.[6]

[6]For a more detailed explanation, see Omote and Yano (2020).

2 Money and Its Function

What role does money play in the economy? It is important to address this question before discussing the role of virtual currency. Money has three basic functions: a scale of value, a medium of exchange, and a store of value.

A transaction is an activity to set conditions for an exchange and then to carry out the exchange. To make an exchange, it is necessary to evaluate what value a particular good has. For such an evaluation, a scale of value is necessary against which the good can be measured. It is necessary that a scale must allow for the four arithmetic operations of addition, subtraction, multiplication, and division; without this capability, no two goods can be measured against each other.

A medium of exchange means the function that synchronizes the timing of transactions. Think of a person who expects to acquire a lot of apples tomorrow and wants to exchange some apples for oranges. He happens to meet a person today who has a lot of oranges and has to leave the town tonight. Money facilitates an exchange in such a case; the person who will soon have apples can pay money for oranges, and the other person can spend the money he receives to buy apples later. This is an example showing that money, as a medium of exchange, fixes the intertemporal misalignment of transaction opportunities. Next, think of three people who live in totally different places and cannot meet at one place; the first is an orange eater owning apples, the second is a grape eater with oranges, and the third is an apple eater with grapes. In this state, it is extremely difficult for each person to get what he/she likes by exchanging goods. Money can facilitate an exchange in such a case as well. If, for example, the orange eater has money, he can buy oranges from the grape eater (second person), who has oranges. The grape eater can use this money to buy grapes from the apple eater (third person), who owns grapes. Finally, the apple eater can use the money to buy apples from the orange eater (first person), who owns apples. In this way, money returns to the first person, who initially owned it; everyone gets what he/she wants to eat. This is an example showing that money, as a medium of exchange, fixes the spatial misalignment of transaction opportunities. These examples show that money can serve as a medium of exchange because everyone knows that others accept money for goods.

As a store of value, money lets its owner save purchasing power until the need emerges to purchase goods and services. This is a function that a medium of exchange must possess to fix the misalignment of transaction opportunities. A material that is highly perishable, such as ice cream, can never serve as a medium of exchange.

To use a particular good as money, it must possess all three functions of money. Since diamonds are wanted by everyone and do not decay, they are good for a medium of exchange and a store of value. However, diamonds are not suitable for the four arithmetic operations. If a diamond were divided into two pieces, its value would substantially decrease. The divided pieces cannot be put back together. This implies that diamonds are unsuitable as a scale of value.

Radioactive substances such as uranium may be good for a scale of value and a store of value. However, it is too dangerous to carry around in small portions, which implies that uranium cannot serve as a medium of exchange. Iron is very good for a scale of value and a medium of exchange. However, iron rusts too quickly to be a store of value in comparison with copper, which explains why, historically, copper coins have been more common than iron coins.

3 Transaction Costs and Money

History shows that a new type of money was, and is right now, introduced when it can economize the existing transaction costs by raising trust in money.[7] This has contributed to the creation of an economy with a higher quality market economy. In this section, I will examine this process.

3.1 Commodity Money

What materials are good for money? The first answer that comes to mind is precious metals such as gold and silver. Because everyone wants these precious metals and can carry them in small portions, it is perfect as a medium of exchange. Because those precious metals do not lose their values easily, they are good for a store of value. Moreover, these metals can easily be divided into small pieces and melted into a big chunk. This implies that they are good for the four arithmetic operations.

One problem of these precious metals is that they are too precious. This implies that they are not suitable for small transactions. Copper is a metal that is more suitable for small transactions. Because copper does not rust as quickly as iron, copper coins have been widely used for many centuries. In addition, copper has been in daily use for tools and ornaments.

Previously, real goods such as silk, barley, or rice were used as a medium of exchange. Although they are far more fragile than precious metals, it may be that they were more acceptable for many ordinary traders as a medium of exchange in the world in which gold, silver, and copper were not readily available.

3.2 Currency and Transaction Costs

Unlike commodity money, there are types of money the value of which is not directly linked to the use of goods. That is the currency. Whether it is a banknote or a ledger currency, its value stems from the fact that they are accepted as money by people. In other words, a currency plays the role of money supported by the trust of the

---

[7] For market quality theory, see Yano (2019), which focuses on different types of transaction costs for newly developing markets.

people. As discussed above, how trust in currency is created differs between paper money, deposit currencies, and virtual currencies. Paper money is backed up by a government's monetary policy, deposit currencies are backed by the operation of banks, and virtual currencies are backed by decentralized algorithms.

A shift away from commodity money to a currency may be explained by a reduction of the transaction cost associated with the use of commodity money. If rice or silk is used as a means of exchange, its quality as a commodity can deteriorate easily; rice could become inedible; silk could become worn out. The value of gold and silver does not deteriorate easily. However, they are too precious for small transactions and can become an easy target for robbers.

This explains why paper money was invented as soon as a precious-metal standard was established. Deposit currencies were adopted to economize costs of handling cash.

As this shows, a currency has been developed to economize transaction costs. In other words, a choice of a currency is determined by a comparison in transaction cost between the existing money and an alternative currency that may be newly developed.

3.3 Ledger Currencies and Transaction Costs

The cost of maintaining a deposit currency is rather high. This can be easily understood by thinking of the numbers of banks, their branches, and people working there. Many people are excited about virtual currencies because they expect virtual currencies to economize that cost significantly. This may be explained by comparing a traditional encyclopedia and Wikipedia.

Previously, many families had a set of encyclopedias, in which experts explain their respective subjects, covering social phenomena, historical facts, and scientific knowledge. The process of putting an encyclopedia together may be called "centralized knowledge processing" just like centralized network computing. The editorial board of an encyclopedia is responsible for centrally controlling the selection of authors for all subjects. Although all subjects are explained by experts, they are checked by the editorial board, which is responsible for making sure that all explanations are correct and trustworthy. In other words, the editorial board acts as if it is the central server of a centralized network.

In contrast, Wikipedia is based on "decentralized knowledge processing." Every Wikipedia article is written by an expert or multiple experts. However, no authority exists who is trusted to check whether articles are correct. Instead, all users check articles, add explanations, if needed, and correct errors if present.

The decentralized knowledge processing introduced by Wikipedia has its drawbacks. Sometimes, we see some errors in an explanation because there is no centralized trusted authority that checks the articles. Some explanations are too technical for ordinary people to understand.

A strong merit of Wikipedia is to utilize human altruism or the urge to share information accurately to build something useful for the society. If you have the charitable mindset to share accurate information with society, and you have confidence in your expertise, you will be tempted to write an article for Wikipedia. It requires considerable effort for a person to write an article that ordinary people can understand. If you write a fake article, someone else will soon find out and rewrite it. This minimizes the incentive to contribute wrong and/or inaccurate information.

In short, Wikipedia has effectively utilized the human urge to explain and share knowledge. Thanks to this mechanism, it has succeeded in creating a decentralized encyclopedia with a huge content at a very small cost.

In many respects, blockchain is similar to Wikipedia. It does not use a centralized management system. Except for setting the minimum protocol, there is no centralized control, and the evaluation of information is decentralized and left to a large number of anonymous participants. It maximizes the willingness of well-meaning people to make accurate records and decentralizes the protection against malicious attacks. Through such design, virtual currencies offer money at a lower cost than the expensive system of centralized deposit currencies.

3.4 Cost Structure of Different Currencies

Figure 1 illustrates the difference between paper money and ledger currencies and that between deposit and virtual currencies. For each plot, the vertical axis represents the price of money. The price of money is represented by the nominal interest rate. The left-most panel explains the cost (marginal cost) of paper money in relation to its price. The cost of printing a bill can be assumed to be negligible. No matter how many dollar bills are printed, the cost of printing an additional bill may be assumed to be constant. The price of paper money is determined at a level much higher than the marginal cost.

In the middle and right-most panels of Fig. 1, the marginal cost curve for creating a ledger currency is an upward-sloping line. This is because the additional cost of increasing the currency supply, either in deposit or virtual currency, becomes larger

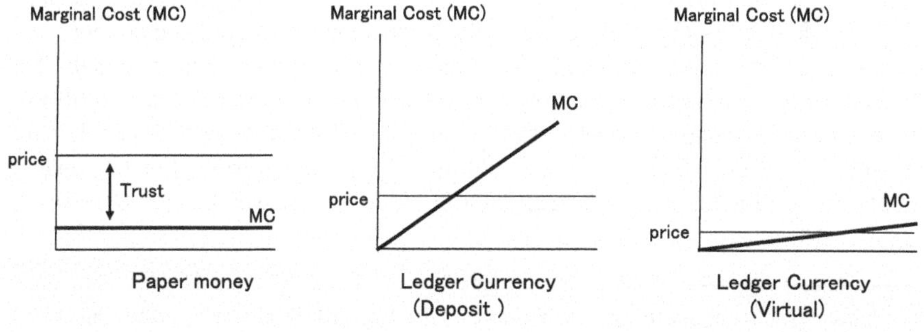

Fig. 1 Cost structure of currencies

as the supply increases. However, as noted above, it may be assumed that the cost of creating a virtual currency is much smaller.

In these simple cases, it is known that the marginal cost curve and the supply curve are identical. Therefore, as shown in the middle and right panels, the supply of a ledger currency is determined at the intersection between the price of a currency and the marginal cost curve. In contrast, as the left-most panel of the figure shows, in the case of paper money, the supply of a currency is determined by the government's monetary policy; there is no relationship between the unit price of money and the marginal cost curve.

4 New Monetary Theory for the Digital Era

To explain the use of virtual currencies economically, it is necessary to create a new monetary theory that shows what the difference in cost structure in Fig. 1 means.[8] The following provides a brief explanation of this theory. For this purpose, it is useful to return to the Japanese history of money, the overview of which is provided in Sect. 1 of this chapter. This is because, for more than a thousand years, the Japanese monetary system has evolved rather naturally without being disturbed by foreign influences.

4.1 An Economy with Commodity Money Only

As explained in Sect. 1 of this chapter, copper coins were introduced to Japan from the twelfth century through to the middle of the sixteenth century. During that period, Chinese copper coins and gold were used as a medium of exchange along with real goods such as silk and rice.[9]

To describe this system, the left-hand side panel of Fig. 2 illustrates the market for gold, and the right-hand side panel shows that for copper coins. The vertical axis represents the unit prices of gold and copper coins in units of goods and services, which are denoted as Q and P, respectively. If the supplies of gold and copper coins are assumed to be fixed, they can be illustrated by vertical lines in those panels. The demands for gold and copper coins are illustrated by curves G and C. The equilibrium prices for gold and copper coins are determined at the intersections between demand and supply curves, which are Q for gold and P for copper coins. For the sake of simplicity, assume that the exchange rate of gold to copper was 1–4 (or $Q = 4P$).

---

[8]For conventional monetary theory, see Niehans (1978), Iwai (1993), Kiyotaki and Wright (1989), and Rocheteau and Wright (2005).

[9]The use of goods such as rice, cotton, dye, and silk as money has been recorded since the eighth century. See Takizawa (1996, p. 2).

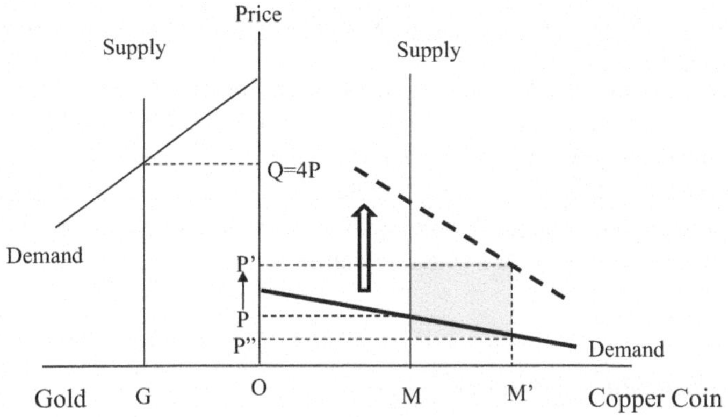

Fig. 2 Real commodity money and Nobunaga's alchemy

4.2 *Nobunaga Oda's Currency Policy*

Nobunaga Oda (1534–1582) was a feudal lord who almost unified Japan towards the end of a warring period of more than one hundred years(1467–1587). After his death, his conquest was succeeded by one of his leading generals, Hideyoshi Toyotomi, who united the entirety of Japan in 1587.

It is arguable that Nobunaga Oda is the first person who tried and succeeded in converting the commodity money economy into a currency economy in Japan. Oda actively promoted the use of copper coins; his battle flag had three pictures of a Ming Dynasty Chinese coin called Eiraku-tsuho.[10] In 1569, Oda adopted the law stipulating the exchange rates for gold, silver, and copper coins at 1 ryo (about 16.5 grams) of gold equal to 7.5 ryo of silver and to 1.5 kanmon of copper coins (mon is the basic counter for copper coins and 1000 mon is 1 kanmon).[11]

More importantly, Oda set the exchange rates among various grades of copper coins.[12] At that time all sorts of copper coins circulated, including old Japanese coins, those imported through Song and Ming trade, and privately minted coins from both China and Japan. The imported copper coins included Tang, Song, and Ming dynasty coins even during the Ming period.[13] Many of those coins were broken in half and worn out. It is documented that before Oda, there were many quarrels because of refusals to accept those low copper coins. Oda sets four grades copper, including

[10]See https://samurai-world.com/oda-nobunagas-crests/.

[11]A record exists as early as the first half of the eighth century that the government set an exchange rate between silver coins and copper coins; see Takizawa (1996, p. 3). Before Oda, various local lords set exchange rates between different grades of copper coins. Nobunaga Oda's innovation is that he set an exchange rate between gold (bullion) and copper coins; see Takizawa (1996, Chap. 3) and Takagi (2016, Chap. 2).

[12]See Okuno (1969, pp. 256, 257).

[13]For example, the majority of the excavated old coins are Song dynasty coins with some Tang and Ming coins. See Takizawa (1996, p. 63, Table 4).

broken coins (third degree) and privately minted (fourth degree) and related their values to that of gold.[14]

Nobunaga Oda defeated many feudal lords and in doing so he collected large quantities of gold, silver, and copper coins. As explained in the next section, Oda's policy was to create a currency, from which he obtained a large amount of purchasing power. We refer to this policy as Oda's alchemy. Before describing this policy, the reader must appreciate that the following discussion is purely a theory that may or may not reflect Nobunaga Oda's actual intention.

4.3 "Nobunaga's Alchemy"

To describe the effect of Nobunaga Oda's policy back in the sixteenth century, we consider a fictitious world that is ruled by an absolute monarch called "Nobunaga." He possesses a large number of gold and copper coins. Everyone knows that he never breaks his promises. The economy before Nobunaga is described by Fig. 2; the exchange ratio of gold and copper is four copper coins to one unit of gold ($Q = 4P$). In that economy, copper coins and gold are not highly substitutable. Those who use copper coins for transactions are basically separated from those who use gold for transactions. There are many people who only use copper coins. They are vaguely aware of the exchange rate between copper coins to gold. However, they do not know if and where they can actually exchange their copper coins for gold at the exchange rate. Under these circumstances, it can be assumed that the price of copper coins primarily reflects the use of copper as a commodity.

Suppose that, in this state, Nobunaga raises his official value of copper coins to one unit of gold for two copper coins ($Q = 2P$). This revaluation of copper coins implies that gold has become cheaper. If Nobunaga were an ordinary, untrustworthy lord, a large amount of gold would leave his hands because people would substitute copper coins for gold. A large volume of copper coins would consequently accumulate in the hands of Nobunaga. The price of copper coins would fall, which would make it impossible to support the artificially raised price of copper coins.

If, however, Nobunaga were an absolute ruler, and people trust whatever Nobunaga says, then he can raise a large volume of funds with which he can purchase goods, soldiers, and other workers. Why?

Because people hold copper coins to use as a medium of exchange and because they believe that Nobunaga will never break his promise. If people trust that he will never break his promise, as money, copper coins are just as good as, or even better than, gold. As a usual commodity, of course, copper is still not as valuable as gold. As a scale of value, however, they will become exactly the same.

[14]Nobunaga Oda was not the first to introduce a rule on low-quality coins. However, historians report that he was the first to determine clear exchange rates between low-quality coin; see Takizawa (1996).

Assume that before Nobunaga revalues copper coins, copper coins and gold served different purposes as a medium of exchange; copper coins were for daily goods whereas gold was for highly valuable goods. People who used copper coins for transactions did not know how and where they could exchange their copper coins for gold; they knew only vaguely that gold was much more valuable than copper coins.

Once the fictitious ruler revalues copper coins and declares that he will exchange copper coins for gold at the declared rate, two copper coins will become the same as one unit of gold as a store of value. Both as a medium of exchange and as a store of value, copper coins will become more valuable than one half unit of gold because copper coins have now become twice as valuable as before and because Nobunaga's guarantee on the exchange rate reduces the uncertainty that copper coins were subject to in the previous economy. To simplify this explanation, we assume that the revaluation of copper coins will not affect the gold market, illustrated on the left-hand side panel. That is, the price of gold will stay at Q.

All these suggest that we may safely assume that after the revaluation, the demand (willingness to pay) for copper coins will become more than twice as much as before. In Fig. 2, the new demand for money is illustrated under the assumption that the demand becomes three times as high; that is, the dotted curve is three times as high as the original demand curve on the right-hand side panel.

Then, the upward shift of the money demand curve will create an excess demand for copper coins. Because people believe that Nobunaga will honor his promise to exchanging one unit of gold for two copper coins, he will be able to keep his promise to maintain the price of copper coins at $P' = 2P$ by releasing his copper coins, of which we assume that he owns many. At P', the demand for copper coins is M'. Thus, he will raise money by as much as $2P'(M' - M)$, which he can then use to purchase goods and soldiers. This is what we call "Nobunaga's alchemy."

If Nobunaga were not to conduct the "alchemy" and released copper coins by as much as $M' - M$, the price of copper coins would fall along the original money demand curve to P''. In this respect, the gain from the "alchemy" may be thought of as $(P' - P'')(M' - M)$.

4.4 *Monetary Policy of Nobunaga Oda and Hideyoshi Toyotomi*

As the above analysis shows, what makes "Nobunaga's alchemy" possible is the trust that he enjoys from people. This trust is the source that turns totally valueless materials, such as worn-out copper coins, into something as valuable as gold.

A historical fact is that in 1569, Nobunaga Oda adopted his exchange rates of gold, silver, and various grades of copper coins at 1 ryo of gold = 7.5 ryo of silver = 1.5 kanmon of copper coins. It is known that before this policy was introduced, it was recorded that 1 ryo of gold equaled 10 ryo of silver and 2 kanmon of bronze coins. If the latter exchange rates were held until Nobunaga Oda's days, his 1569 policy is a revaluation of silver and copper coins against gold.[15]

To implement such a policy, it is absolutely important that people believed that Oda could keep his promise unconditionally. To create such a trust, what did Oda need to do?

The answer would be to let people know that he had a huge amount of gold to back up his promise. In fact, it is known that the top floor of his castle, built in 1578 and visible to everyone, was plated with gold (Frois 1593). Hideyoshi Toyotomi, who took over Oda's position after he was killed in 1582, announced that he would maintain Oda's monetary policy. He then revalued the low grade copper coins by setting 1 ryo of gold equal to 2 kanmon of low grade coins; in contrast, Oda had set 1 ryo of gold equal to 1.5 kanmon of high quality gold coins.

Toyotomi built the famous golden portable tea house used to entertain the emperor and he invited town people for tea at the tea house set in a big Kyoto shrine. The large gold coins that Toyotomi minted were for gifts and it was well known that he owned a huge amount of gold. It makes a lot of sense if the purpose of Nobunaga and Toyotomi's showy use of gold was to gain people's trust in the currency (copper coins) that they wanted to use effectively.

4.5 Paper Money System

The theory of currency creation in the previous section assumes the existence of two types of goods. One of them is a real good that is intrinsically more valuable than the other good, which is to be used as a currency. The theory shows that a trusted government can create a currency (and profit from it) by revaluating the less valuable commodity against the more valuable one. This captures a general feature on creation of all types of currencies except virtual currency.

Figure 2 may be interpreted as a model capturing the gold standard system. For that purpose, it suffices simply to reinterpret the right-hand side panel as a market for paper money.

It is also possible to interpret Fig. 2 as a model of the fiat money system. For that interpretation, the left-hand side panel may be thought of as a market for financial assets. Under the Glass–Steagall Act, private banks and securities houses were, respectively, restricted to participate only in the money market and the securities market. The central bank was, in contrast, the only financial institution that was permitted to participate in both markets. The value of a currency (paper money) was controlled by the central bank, which was, and still is, authorized to intervene in both markets. If, just like "Nobunaga" in Fig. 2, the central bank can fix the exchange rate of paper money against financial assets within a certain range, the fiat money system can be sustained. Such a policy has been called an open market operation, which we do not often hear about anymore (Fig. 3).

[15]See Takagi (2016, p. 74).

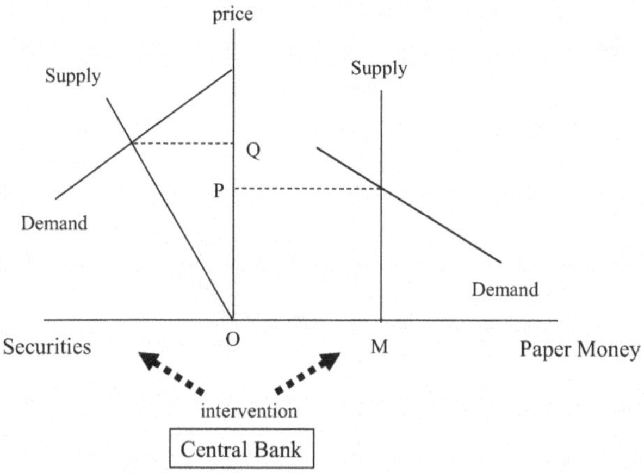

Fig. 3 Fiat Money and Glass-Steagall

The Glass–Steagall Act, which separated the stock market and the currency market, was abolished in 1999. This stopped any restriction on combining the money market and the financial market. Because the institutional separation between banks and securities firms was lost, the financial market has become a place for a two-player money game between the central banks and private financial institutions. Without going into great detail, it may be considered that the repeal of the Glass–Steagall Act led to the Global Financial Crisis in 2008. In this respect, it is understandable that the birth of Bitcoin is attributed to the financial crisis as discussed in Chapter 3.

4.6 Deposit Currency to Virtual Currency

The modern economy is built on a financial system based on banknotes and deposit currencies. Is it possible to convert it to an economy based on virtual currency?

To answer this question, it is necessary first to describe the economy with both paper money and a deposit currency. For this purpose, in Fig. 4, the marginal cost curve of the deposit currency is drawn as a straight upward curve starting from M in the figure. If the amount of paper money is M, then the supply of the entire currency is also indicated by the same straight line. If the deposit currency is provided to an economy where only banknotes circulate, the unit price of the currency will drop from P to P'.

According to economic theory, the benefits that the whole economy receives from money creation are indicated by the area between the demand curve and the supply curve. In other words, the introduction of a deposit currency into the economy with only paper money (described in Fig. 2) benefits the society by the area of the light-gray triangle.

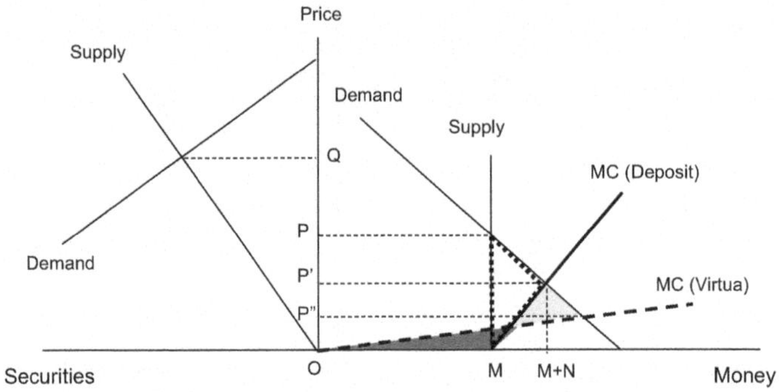

Fig. 4 Deposit and virtual currency equilibria

Next, let us focus on the marginal cost of a virtual currency shown by the dotted line in Fig. 4. Now suppose that the monetary system shifted from using currency and paper money to one using only virtual currency. In that case, the equilibrium is determined at the intersection of the currency demand curve and the marginal cost curve of the virtual currency. As the figure shows, this shift benefits the economy by the light-gray triangle in the figure and harms it by the dark-gray triangle.

In Fig. 4, the marginal cost curve of the virtual currency is drawn in such a way that the areas of these two triangles are equal to each other. This implies that if the marginal cost curve of the virtual currency is lower than the dotted line, switching to the virtual currency system will benefit the whole of society.

In short, if a virtual currency can economize the transaction cost necessary to maintain deposit currencies sufficiently, it can take over the entire currency system. If that happens in the future, an economy without a central banking system will develop.

References

Frois L (1593). Historia de Japam, available in Japanese translation, Nihonshi, 12 vols, translated by Matsuda and Kawasaki, Chuoukoronsha
Iwai, K (1993) Monetary theory, in Japanese, Kaheiron, Chikuma
Kiyotaki N, Wright R (1989) On money as a medium of exchange. J Polit Econ
Mikami R (1996) The story of money in Edo, in Japanese, Edo no KaheiMonogatari, Toyokeizai
Niehans J (1978) The theory of money
Okuno T (1969) Research on Nobunaga Oda documents, vol. 1, in Japanese, Oda Nobunaga Bunsho no Kenkyu, Jou, Yoshikawa Kobunkan
Rocheteau G, Wright R (2005). Money in search equilibrium, in competitive equilibrium, and in competitive search equilibrium. Econometrica
Takagi H (2016) Japanese history of currencies, in Japanese, Tshuuka no Nihonshi, Chuoukoronsha
Takizawa T (1996) History of the Japanese money, in Japanese, Nihon no Kahei no Rekishi, Nihon Rekishi Gakkai

Yano M (2019) Market quality theory and the Coase theorem in the presence of transaction costs, RIETI DP19-E-097

Makoto Yano is Chairman of the Research Institute of Economy, Trade and Industry (RIETI); he is also a specially appointed professor at Kyoto University, Jochi University, and Chubu University. He is an internationally known researcher who has made a number of substantial contributions in international trade, market theory, and especially on economic dynamics. His contributions in economic dynamics, for example, are represented by articles in *Econometrica* in 1995 and the *Journal of Economic Theory* in 1996, which explained the conditions under which general economic equilibrium shows chaotic behavior. His 1998 *Econometrica* article is recognized as the latest most important work on the characterization of dynamic general equilibrium.

Besides those rather theoretical works, Prof. Yano has also provided influential insights on contemporary real-world phenomena. Those include transfer problems (*American Economic Review*, 1999), voluntary export restraints (*International Economic Review* [IER], 1995), and trade conflicts (IER, 1998), on which there have been a number of follow-up papers.

His recent research on "market quality" addresses various problems in modern economies, including the financial market crisis since 2008 and the recent nuclear accidents in Japan, from the point of view of market quality—a new economic concept that Prof. Yano has developed and is applying to Japanese and international markets. Concerning quality of competition, quality of information, and quality of products, market quality is defined as an index jointly determined by the efficiency of an allocation and the fairness of the prices that are achieved in a market. Prof. Yano received a B.A. in economics from The University of Tokyo in 1971 and a Ph.D. in economics from The University of Rochester in 1981.

Chapter 5
Ethereum, Smart Contracts, DApps

William Metcalfe

On February 28, 2012, an 18-year-old high school student wrote "If Bitcoin is to achieve mainstream success, it cannot stop at the limited crowds of Internet geeks, libertarians, and privacy advocates that it is hitting now, and it must find some way to attract the mainstream public (Buterin 2012)." At the time, 1 Bitcoin was worth 4.87 USD or 400 JPY. The Initial Coin Offering (ICO) did not exist. Ethereum was not yet even a proposal.

Whether you consider Bitcoin to be mainstream might depend on where you fall on the adoption curve, but the fact that you are reading this now means Bitcoin has most certainly reached beyond the "limited crowds of Internet geeks." The author of that quote was Vitalik Buterin in one of his early articles for *Bitcoin Magazine*. We will look at his role and contributions shortly. First, however, we consider how we arrived at the world of blockchain and DApps, starting with the concept of decentralization.

1 A Brief History of Decentralization

Decentralization is a fundamental part of the clever solution that gave us Bitcoin, the first widely successful digital currency. For currencies we know well, like Japanese Yen or US Dollars, or even other types of "currencies" such as customer loyalty points or air miles, we rely on a single authority like a central bank, an issuing

This article has been prepared for the study group "Blockchain and Society 5.0—The Creation of a New Marketplace based on Distributed Consensus" at the Research Institute of Economy, Trade, and Industry (RIETI) . I would like to thank RIETI and the study group for including me in this project as well as Makoto Yano, Chris Dai, and Jeff Wentworth for their gracious support and input throughout the process.

W. Metcalfe (✉)
Curvegrid, Tokyo, Japan
e-mail: william@curvegrid.com

M. Yano et al. (eds.), *Blockchain and Crypto Currency*,
Economics, Law, and Institutions in Asia Pacific,
https://doi.org/10.1007/978-981-15-3376-1_5

company, or another trusted custodian to guarantee the value of our money. Bitcoin does away with the need for a central authority by dividing the responsibility of protecting the network amongst the participants. But decentralization is as old as currency itself.

Gold used to be used as a decentralized currency because it too can be used without referring to a central authority. Someone can trade gold for goods and services with both parties recognizing its value. It has utility as a compact and fungible store of that value. Because of the similarity in concept, many describe Bitcoin as "digital gold" and Satoshi Nakamoto's famous paper uses the metaphor of mining, just like gold, to describe the creation of new coins (Nakamoto 2009).[1]

Of course, decentralization does not belong only to currencies. Modern Western democracy, created in ancient Athens and developed through the French and American revolutions, is practiced by the world's most advanced economies. It is our most familiar form of decentralization.

Computation also uses the pattern of decentralization outside of blockchain. NASA, for example, designed its space flight computers to be redundant by allowing multiple systems to vote on the output of a computation (National Aeronautics and Space Administration 1971). If one makes a mistake, the other computers will override it by majority.

It took, however, quite some time for decentralization and currency to rejoin forces since the retirement of gold as a day-to-day medium of exchange. The Knights Templar, a medieval Catholic military order, are often credited with inventing modern banking (Harford 2017). Twelfth century pilgrims would deposit their valuables with the Templars and receive a paper letter indicating the entitled value. Carrying the *promise* of gold was much more efficient and secure than carrying actual gold. Those promises are not too different from the currencies and instruments we use today.

Blockchain brings another type of efficiency to those promises by obviating the need for the Templars (or any other third party) by purely using technology. The first to use that technology successfully was Bitcoin. It allows a simple peer-to-peer value exchange from one account to another.

2 Ethereum

Vitalik Buterin became interested in Bitcoin at the encouragement of his father. After researching Bitcoin, he began writing articles in exchange for the cryptocurrency and started *Bitcoin Magazine* with another colleague. Eventually he had the revelation that the platform could become very powerful by being generalized beyond simple currency exchange into something that could perform *any* type of processing.

[1] Satoshi Nakamoto is well known to be an alias and the identity of the real author is unknown. L.S., "Who is Satoshi Nakamoto?", 2015, https://www.economist.com/the-economist-explains/2015/11/02/who-is-satoshi-nakamoto.

It may be easy to think of Bitcoin as a computer network that replaces your bank. But it is a little trickier to imagine how adding complex processing to Bitcoin could be useful. So let us approach it from the opposite angle and imagine your bank as a type of computer. It has three instructions: deposit money to my account, withdraw money from my account, send money from my account to another account.

Now imagine if you could give your bank special instructions to accomplish your savings goals: "for the next year, only allow me to withdraw up to 100 dollars per week." Or suppose you wanted to create a shared account for your startup business where the CEO has full control but wants an extra level of accountability for the other officers. "Make an account with three owners. Alice can withdraw as much as she wants anytime but Bob and Charles can only withdraw funds if one of the others also approves."

You could even automate the distribution of proceeds from your business "every time 20 dollars or more is deposited to the account, give 5 each to Alice, Bob, and Charles, and divide the remainder evenly amongst all other accounts on a special list." Each of those accounts might have its own special instructions! Maybe Bob wants all the funds to go directly to his favorite charity.

These are simple examples but something that would be really difficult to achieve with an actual bank because of the number of humans and processes involved; they are not equipped to provide that level of customization. It would involve power of attorney with someone you really trust, a series of elaborate legal contracts and independent bookkeeping, or all of the above. With a few lines of software, those examples can be created and the pattern replicated to anyone else who wishes to accomplish the same outcome.

It was possible that Bitcoin could evolve into this limitless computer. The developers with whom Buterin was working, however, were not receptive to this grand idea so he decided to embark upon the project himself. Thus, Ethereum was conceived around 2014 and launched in 2015 to extend the concept of Bitcoin. Ethereum has its own currency Ether (ETH) , just like Bitcoin (BTC), but the platform can run any set of instructions, not just "send and receive Bitcoin (Hacket 2016)."

2.1 Smart Contracts

Back in 1994, Nick Szabo, a computer scientist and legal scholar, created the term "smart contract" and defined it as: "A smart contract is a computerized transaction protocol that executes the terms of a contract (Szabo 1994)." He envisioned a way of bringing efficiency to written agreements in a way that enforces them automatically. Think of a vending machine. Without a shop clerk, it enforces the contract of selling a beverage at an advertised price to the customer who inserts a sufficient amount of money into the machine.

The Turing-complete (Wikipedia contributors 2019) computer engine provided by Ethereum is the first computerized transaction protocol that does many of the things Szabo was envisioning in his earlier writings. Computer programs that are run on the Ethereum platform are called smart contracts. They can enforce *certain types* of agreements between parties, just like a vending machine, but they have no intrinsically direct relationship with legal contracts. The Ethereum smart contract became so popular that the Ethereum version of a smart contract has eclipsed the original use of the term and added a lot of confusion as to what blockchain can do.

Why is it a "contract"? The original idea was that it constituted some kind of agreement between parties. Why is it "smart"? The original idea was that it could execute itself without the need for lawyers or people to be involved. So what is a smart contract really? Since Ethereum declared itself "a decentralized platform that runs smart contracts," it really just refers to a special type of software program. It may or may not have legal implications and still needs a traditional legal framework around it if it needs to be used as part of a legal transaction. For example, if you write a smart contract to securitize real estate, dividing ownership of a property up into virtual tokens, you still need traditional legal contracts (in the appropriate jurisdictions) to tie those smart contract tokens to the actual property.

3 What Is a DApp?

What is it that emerges from the ability to manipulate numbers and data in a trustless manner provided by smart contracts and what would we call such an application? We can now decouple the application from an individual company or owner and create a "decentralized application" also known by the contraction DApp. It can be pronounced with two syllables as "dee-app" or with one syllable as "dapp." Capitalization is not always consistent (as in Dapp) and the D is occasionally written with Đ (as in Đapp), where Đ is the Norse letter eth (ETH News).

Decentralized applications are often described as trustless or peer-to-peer with the distinguishing characteristic that there is no single server or entity controlling it like in a client–server model. We understand the attractive properties of the smart contract and the flexibility of the platform. But to understand what really makes a DApp different from a centralized application, it is worthwhile considering what goes into a contemporary centralized application.

A prototypical modern software application includes at least one user interface (UI); this could be a mobile app downloaded from an app store, a website (accessed from a computer or mobile device), or a desktop application installed on a computer. It usually involves data. This data could be provided by a single group or company, like a weather app using a national weather organization, or like in a social networking app it could be provided by the end users themselves. Finally, it involves some sort of manipulation of the data or computation.

A DApp uses the blockchain at the core of its data storage and processing. This is implemented using a smart contract. Currently the UI for a DApp is usually created using a traditional website model. So one can think of a complete DApp as a website plus one or more smart contracts. A DApp has the same general properties as a traditional application. The main difference, therefore, is that the data and computation are provided by the blockchain.

3.1 DApp and Blockchain

The merit of using blockchains for DApps are as follows:

1. A user can see what is going to happen before executing a function or submitting any data.
2. Once the user has performed an interaction, it cannot be withdrawn, tampered with, or deleted.

By themselves these properties are useful. This embodies decentralization at a protocol level. However, this facilitates another type of decentralization that is a driving philosophical motivation behind DApps:

3. Governance can be decentralized so that the users of the application participate directly in its management.

   At this point, we consider two examples—one makes use of the first two properties, and another that helps demonstrate the idea of governance, or structural, decentralization.

CryptoKitties is one of the more famous decentralized applications (Bowles 2017). It is a game created by Axiom Zen that allows players to trade, breed, collect, and sell virtual cats. Unique or scarce tradeable items are a well-used pattern in gaming, both traditional and digital; however, in CryptoKitties, the virtual items are recorded on the blockchain. In this way, the actions are transparent and guaranteed, but there is nothing particularly decentralized about the ethos of the application.

Another example of a DApp is the DAO (decentralized autonomous organization) (Securities and Exchange Commission 2017). The application was governed by tradeable tokens that had voting rights. In this sense, the mechanism of the application was guaranteed by the decentralized Ethereum layer, but the concept itself was designed for decentralization of authority.

3.2 Coins, Tokens, and DApps

The terms "coin", "token" , "cryptocurrency", "virtual currency" , "digital currency" and, more recently, "crypto asset" are now frequently used in similar or interchangeable ways. We could continue to generate similarly exotic terminology by pairing different "crypto" adjectives with different "coin" synonyms! It is enough to confound even the most diligent financial linguist. Therefore, it may be quite some time before we all agree on the correct language to use, both casually and legally. For now, however, we take a practical approach. We can break apart the different types of technologies and categorize them by the most accepted terms even though there may be some overlap in real world usage.

The primary distinction we will make is between "coins" and "tokens." We can describe coins as a base currency. When a network, such as Bitcoin, includes the currency as an integral part of the software, we think of that currency, in this case Bitcoin, as a coin. As we know, Bitcoin was created for the primary purpose of storing and exchanging funds. In Ethereum, the currency Ether is also built into the platform and is therefore a coin. This applies to other platforms derived from Bitcoin such as Litecoin or Monero. Coins are also used to incentivize good behavior and secure the platform. Coins are used to pay for computation and storage resources and are given to mining nodes as rewards for their work.

We can describe tokens as the units built on top of one of these base networks as a secondary feature. They are a way to take advantage of a robust and established blockchain network to create new digital assets. There is no need to convince users to join a new network or run new software. The token runs on and is secured by an existing network.

One of the earliest attempts to do this was with "colored coins" on Bitcoin (Bradbury 2013). Think of it like taking a poker chip and marking it with a special red stamp. It is still difficult to make a forgery, but now you can use it for another purpose, like a coupon for a free bowl of ramen. Mastercoin (which became Omni) was another attempt to extend Bitcoin by storing extra data along with the native Bitcoin transfer transactions (Buterin 2013). These were both creative attempts to leverage the technology but have some inherent difficulties in aligning with a platform that has its own independent design goals. Bitcoin, for example, introduced an upgrade to reduce the number of tiny transactions. This was done to prevent malicious degradation of the network, however, colored coins are optimized to minimize cost by making use of such tiny transactions.

Ethereum, having been designed from the ground up as a platform for running arbitrary computer programs, lent itself naturally to the creation of tokens on top of its platform. Using an Ethereum smart contract, a software developer can (comparatively) easily create a token with any amount of supply, distribution goals, or custom logic. The Ethereum smart contract formed the basis for most of what we call tokens today.

Tokens, like coins, do not have any innate properties besides their bookkeeping ability. However, they have a few basic genres under which they commonly fall. You may have heard the terms "utility token" or "security token." The reason this distinction is made has to do with how the tokens are used to raise capital for a project or business. Anyone can create tokens from nothing and sell them. The way Ethereum raised money for its development was by selling the platform's future currency (Ether) for Bitcoin. The concept was that Ether could be used to pay for the submission, storage, and execution of smart contracts and related data. It was this "utility" that would make it valuable in the future and a worthwhile investment. It could, of course, also be used simply as a medium of exchange like Bitcoin.

Inspired by the success of Ethereum, many other projects raised money by selling their own tokens. The sale of fractional ownership in a project to the public to raise funds, in exchange for a promise of a share of the future profits, is an economic practice dating back hundreds of years. The potential for defrauding or disappointing investors by lying about a project's potential, absconding with the money, or simply failing to execute, means we have sophisticated laws and regulations in economically advanced societies to prevent good people from being duped into funding bad projects.

Selling cryptocurrency-based tokens proved to be an attractive way to raise a lot of money compared with traditional financing. ICO funding reached a peak in the first quarter of 2018 where blockchain startups raised an astronomical $6.9 billion through ICOs compared with $0.5 billion through equity funding (CB Insights 2019). To avoid running afoul of existing securities laws, many projects took great pains to indicate the tokens they were selling were utility tokens and therefore not subject to existing regulations. There are a number of conflicting legal opinions on the subject. Whether the regulators eventually decide there is a place for utility tokens (and what that place is), the markets as of mid-2019 have had their fill. The span of 2017–2018 was an exceptional period and there is effectively no current interest in such projects (Vigna 2019).

But what about security tokens? A traditional security means attaching a paper or digital legal agreement to a physical object or to a company or project. This could be shares in a company like Toyota or a government bond that pays interest. These types of instruments are things that could be easily modelled or represented in the blockchain. If we allow tokens to represent securities, we can draw on the advantages of tokens, such as broad access to capital with low management overhead, with the reliability and responsibility of legally regulated instruments.

3.3 The Case for DApps

There are a number of applications being pursued in the DApp space. So far, they mostly fall under the following general areas:

- Fundraising (ICOs)
- Marketplaces including exchanges
- Identify providers—know your customer (KYC) and anti-money laundering (AML)
- Financial services
- Securitization of assets
- Supply chain management
- Gaming.

We now examine some of these applications.

To provide financial or securities services like a bank or stock exchange in a pre-DApp world, the barrier to entry is significant. The burdens of regulatory compliance, staff, infrastructure, and institutional relationships required to operate are staggering. In the United States, the estimates to start a bank, for example, are $12 to $20 million in capital (Harrington 2016).

Using a smart contract-based system, where the deposits are governed by publicly visible computer code, anyone with the ability to write software can create a system that securely handles large amounts of assets. An ambitious software developer in 2016 created a working cryptocurrency exchange called EtherDelta (Winters 2016). The exchange smart contract held over a billion dollars of ETH and tokens at its peak.

One of the frequently cited goals of decentralized projects is “self-ownership” of data. After so many security breaches and revelations of large companies selling the personal information of users, DApps provide a chance for users to have more control over their data.

A well-designed smart contract system could allow regulators or lawmakers to authorize or monitor certain activity on a platform. Imagine a sales program where merchants and consumers could register in a marketplace. Each participant would have a unique identity in the program and transactions could be posted and settled directly through the program. Although it might sound undesirable to some less than scrupulous audience members, every transaction could be automatically taxed to the appropriate level by the government. When tax rates change, the government could simply adjust the rate in the smart contract directly and there would be no onerous actions required by merchants to implement the new rates. Moving control to a common system instead of disparate bureaucratic entities has great potential to align societal and commercial interests.

4 Where *Is* the Smart Contract?

Blockchain transactions are stored on a computer, commonly referred to as a node. Popular blockchain platforms such as Ethereum have tens of thousands of nodes operating at any given time. Each node stores an identical copy of all of the transaction records. The node that validates the next batch of transactions, referred to as a block, is called a mining node. The blocks are in turn validated by each mining node.

Every node in the Ethereum network stores a copy of all the software (smart contracts) , data, account balances, and transaction state (Buterin 2014a). If you think that sounds like a lot of data, it is. A copy of the production Ethereum node at the time of writing is about 179 GB of data. A full archive of all transactions that have occurred, including all intermediary states is 1.8 TB.[2] For comparison, a typical smartphone or laptop might have 64–512 GB of total storage.

Transactions are transmitted across the Internet between nodes in a peer-to-peer fashion. That is, nodes have connectivity with some but not all of the nodes in the network. It takes about 40 s for a given transaction to be seen by 95% of the nodes

[2]Running geth version 1.8.18-stable on Ubuntu Linux. https://geth.ethereum.org/.

in the comparable Bitcoin blockchain (Decker and Wattenhofer 2013). A transaction fee is submitted alongside the transaction and the mining node receives the fees for the transactions it groups into the block.

The mining refers to guessing the solution to a mathematical problem (unique to the group of transactions) that cannot be calculated directly. That guessing is done on hardware that can make millions of guesses per second. There is an expected average number of guesses it will take to get to the solution and so the mining node has effectively proven that it has executed a number of guesses. Hence mining is also known as proof-of-work (PoW).

The mined block is distributed back to the network over the Internet and each node will verify all the contained transactions before accepting it and passing it along. Eventually all the nodes will store a copy of the system state that they all agree upon. In this way, it is not so much a distributed computer like one would think of in a traditional sense. It is more like one computer with many clones running in parallel and storing the same information to make sure no one cheats. This is similar to the redundancy of the aforementioned NASA space flight computers but on a much larger scale.

5 DApp Development and Challenges

Ethereum has been around since 2015 and we have only seen a few years of development in the ecosystem. Compare this with some of the early technologies of the Internet. NCSA Mosaic, launched in 1993, was the first graphical browser to popularize the World Wide Web. This was followed by the PHP language, MySQL database, and Apache web server in 1995. These types of tools allowed early technology pioneers such as Amazon and Match.com to create useful applications.

Blogging platforms Blogger, Movable Type, and Wordpress were launched in 1999, 2001, and 2003, respectively. These made it possible for more enthusiasts to participate in the Internet. But it was not until services like Facebook became available and popular that the Internet felt broadly participatory.

5.1 How Are DApps Made?

Many of the tools used to produce and consume DApps are still in their infancy. On the user side of interacting with a DApp, you need a way to create and manage an account on the network. In a traditional application, login information (email and password) is stored on a server. In a DApp, your account is a digital blockchain key stored on your computer's drive or in your smart phone's memory. There are tools to help you manage those keys. The most popular tool to manage DApp (Ethereum) accounts and interact with DApps is MetaMask,[3] an extension for the Chrome, Firefox, and Opera web browsers.

Unlike vanilla web browsers, which automatically upgrade and are relatively stable pieces of software, the new DApp browsers and plugins are often buggy. Furthermore, the new interaction model with DApps including icons, jargon, and actions are still confusing to new users.

There are also popular web-based wallets, such as MyEtherWallet,[4] which allow you to conduct transactions without installing any software. However, it is geared primarily to exchanging Ethereum as a currency and not interacting with DApps. Interacting with a DApp requires you to copy and paste arcane computer code into a web form.

Hardware wallets, such as Trezor[5] and Ledger,[6] are a third type of wallet. They store the encryption keys in a tamper-proof module from which the digital keys cannot be physically removed. That way a user needs to physically connect a device and approve an action. The challenge here is that extra work can be required to set up, understand, and use the device. For DApp and software developers, integrating hardware wallets requires extra development, testing, and consideration.

The aforementioned software and hardware are primarily for end users but are used extensively by developers during the construction of a DApp. There is another suite of tools used only by software developers, including integrated development environments (IDEs) such as Remix, testing frameworks such as Truffle,[7] and the main programming language for Ethereum called Solidity.

Automated testing is another critical component in development. Truffle and its complementary tools Ganache and Drizzle are the main tools used for testing. They let you connect and deploy to a simulated Ethereum network on your own computer to put the smart contract through its paces.

The Ethereum community maintains a series of public test networks as well. In the final stages of development, your smart contract can be deployed to one of these networks for a fully decentralized run-through. Truffle and its components are young like the rest of the toolset and the execution of tests can take more time and effort to run compared with more mature web development frameworks. However, for reasons explained below, thorough testing is an even more critical part of the development cycle when compared with most web applications.

---

[3] https://metamask.io/.

[4] https://www.myetherwallet.com/.

[5] https://trezor.io/.

[6] https://www.ledger.com/.

[7] https://www.truffleframework.com/.

5.2 Smart Contract Maintenance

In the early days of personal computers, most version upgrades took place by purchasing the latest copy of a title and manually installing it. Today, much of the software we use exists as an online web application and is upgraded instantly and transparently by the owner of the website. It is a frequent pattern with contemporary desktop and mobile phone software to enable automatic upgrades. Chrome browser, for example, updates itself by default.

The smart contract upgrade model is unlike either of these models. Ethereum smart contracts are, by design, immutable once deployed. This implies a number of considerations that are very different, even contradictory, to the prevailing philosophies of web development. Consider Facebook's (now retired) motto "Move Fast and Break Things." For the world of smart contracts, one might propose the motto "Move Carefully and Test Thoroughly so Things Never Break."

Much of the community and audience for DApps comes from a web centric background where certain types of rigor have lost favor and been replaced with rapid iteration and disposability. Testing has a prominent role in smart contract development. Besides testing, the rather academic discipline of formal verification has made its way into the blockchain discourse. Techniques used in industrial, mass transit, aerospace, and other fields where mistakes have huge consequences can also be applied. But systems will still need to grow, and, despite the best intentions, mistakes will still be made.

Given that we expect and plan for platforms to evolve, there are a few ways, at least in Ethereum, that one can approach a path for upgrades.

1. The deployed smart contract (contract A) can be a pointer to another smart contract (contract B) that implements the actual functionality. Somewhat like a mail forwarding address. If the functionality needs changing, A's reference to contract B gets updated to point to a replacement (contract C).
2. The smart contract uses replaceable underlying libraries to implement its functionality. This is conceptually similar to the first technique and differs mainly in technical nuances.

Both of these methods allow for a seamless transition to the new system (provided there are no problems or compatibility issues), but it explicitly removes one of the properties that makes smart contracts valuable. You do not know what will happen in the future. In a basic token implementation, will someone rewrite the underlying smart contract so that my assets can now be garnished by a party I may not trust? If it is immutable and non-upgradeable, you can verify with some confidence that your tokens will be secure.

However, there is one more upgrade method that can work even if the deployed smart contract is completely immutable and non-upgradeable.

3. You make a new smart contract and tell everyone to use it instead of the old one.

Take an example of a token backed by copper. The fictional company "Acme Copper Coins" buys a bunch of copper and puts it in a warehouse somewhere. They create a smart contract to issue tokens against their copper supply. But perhaps they underestimated the demand for their tokens and the smart contract was designed to only support up to 30,000 coin buyers.

Acme could make a new smart contract that supports up to 60,000 buyers and declare they are copying your token balances from the old smart contract to the new smart contract. From now on they are no longer going to honor redemptions of the old tokens. This is ostensibly OK because my new token is worth the same as my old token. However, there is a limit to what a blockchain system can directly control. Beyond that limit, we still rely on the instruments and conventions that exist in our present society such as traditional contract law, public reputation, and trust. We still have to trust Acme that they actually have copper in their warehouse and that I can trade in my tokens with them for copper if I want to. Moreover, we might expect the traditional justice system to intervene if they renege on that promise.

6 The Boundary Between DApps and the Real World

DApps are still a developing technology. To be put into wide use, it is necessary to overcome various issues, including consistency with regulations, data reliability, and the ability to respond to expanding demand (scalability) .

6.1 Consistency with Laws

Legal and regulatory frameworks are an important consideration when developing many applications that hope to migrate to the blockchain. Take real estate tokenization for example. If Alice sends a token to Bob that represents a share in a particular piece of property in Tokyo, then that transaction can take place in a way that is guaranteed and verifiable by the technology. Alice could set a price and Bob can see that if he pays that price, the token will reach his custody. Nothing can prevent Alice from withholding the token or Bob from withholding payment. In this example, the blockchain replaces the escrow function of a trusted third party. It does not, however, replace the fact that there needs to be laws that tie the share of property to that digital token.

6.2 Reliability of Data

Getting trustable data into the blockchain is also an issue. Let us say you wanted to create an insurance scheme that would pay out if the temperature gets too cold. Perhaps farmers would pay into this and receive compensation if the temperature drops below a specified threshold. You could create a system where anyone could participate as an underwriter and anybody could participate as a policy holder. Effectively parties would be taking opposite sides of a bet on the weather.

A system that feeds real-world data into the blockchain for use by smart contracts is known as an "oracle." By trusting a smart contract system that depends on an oracle, you are implicitly trusting that oracle as a reliable source of data. If you allow many oracles to provide data in a decentralized manner including incentives for telling the truth and disincentives for cheating, then you can create a more robust system.

Randomness is another piece of complexity in the blockchain worth mentioning. Randomness is used in many cryptographic systems and techniques to guarantee fairness. Because the internals of a smart contract and the participants' attempts to interact with it are visible to the blockchain network, a miner could gain an advantage by knowing or altering the outcome of a transaction. For example, if a smart contract-based lottery for highly coveted tickets to a sporting event relied on seemingly unpredictable data such as the block creation time, the block miner could adjust the publication time to manipulate the result.

6.3 Scalability

Like Bitcoin, Ethereum grew organically as an experiment. As more people join the network, the demands on the technology become higher. Scalability is the potential of the system to meet those growing demands. To frame the topics of scalability it helps to understand the fee structure surrounding transactions and block creation.

Currently the target block creation time, a compromise between security, efficiency, and practical network limitations, is 12 s between blocks (Buterin 2014). To maintain this rate, the mining difficulty is automatically adjusted by the Ethereum software as mining power is added or removed from the network.

As mentioned earlier, users of Ethereum submit a fee when submitting transactions to the network. This fee is measured in units called gas and relates to the size and complexity of the transaction. The miners claim a per-transaction fee as part of their incentive to secure the integrity of the blockchain and the fee structure helps balance the supply and demand for transaction processing.

There is a block gas limit agreed to by mining nodes, which caps the maximum amount of fees that can be accepted into a block. This is used to manage the bandwidth, cost of storage, and cost of computation per block. That gas limit is about 8,000,000 at the time of writing, and with an average transaction size of about 80,000 gas, about 100 transactions will fit in a block. Hence, the network can currently process about 8 transactions per second.[8]

Some of the main topics in scalability are:

- Transaction throughput

[8]https://etherscan.io/.

This is the quantity of transactions (currently 8 per second), such as sending and receiving tokens, that the blockchain network can process per unit of time. This number is often compared with Visa's 24,000 transactions per second (Visa, accessed 26 November 2019). However, we must remember that these systems were made for different purposes and even then, an Ethereum payment transaction is really like payment, clearing, and settlement all in one.

- Computational cost
  Block validation and mining are costly in terms of computer hardware, electricity, and ultimately fees paid by the users of the network as explained above. All the mining nodes in the network perform all the transaction computations and this is inefficient.
- Data storage
  In Ethereum, currently all full participants keep a complete record of all blockchain transactions. Because of the amount of accumulated data in the blockchain, it is untenable on most consumer devices now to run a full Ethereum node.

The areas where blockchain seems slower or less efficient than its nonblockchain counterpart technologies are caused by the trade-offs that enabled it to work in a decentralized manner. There is, of course, active work and research being done to improve real or perceived shortcomings and eliminate obstacles to growth.

Proof-of-stake (PoS) is an alternative to PoW mining systems that will allow a higher transaction rate. Rather than commit computing resources to guessing a mathematical answer to verify a block (as in mining) , users will be able to pledge Ethereum for a period of time to gain voting rights on block confirmation and receive a reward in exchange for helping to secure the integrity of the blockchain network. They cannot use this pledged Ethereum and they could forfeit their stake if they cheat.

The computation work and data storage can be split amongst different groups of nodes. That way both computation and storage can be divided with a sufficient level of redundancy. This technique is known as sharding.

Light nodes are another way that the network becomes more accommodating to different players. Mobile devices, for example, lack the storage capacity to participate in most public blockchains. A light node can contain the data required to perform minimal validation on transactions and act as a conduit to the broader network, relaying data both to and from the client.

6.4 The Future of DApps

We have been looking mostly at Ethereum; however, there are a number of competing technologies being developed of which Ethereum is just one. Not all of these technologies will proliferate. If we look at the late 1980s and early 1990s, Mintel was a popular network in France with similar models attempted around Europe and other parts of the world, while CompuServe existed in the United States. Eventually, both of these services were fully supplanted by the Internet.

However, older technologies do not always disappear just because newer or better technologies emerge. Legacy technologies can continue to exist alongside newer ones. For example, even though voice and video applications such as Skype or Google Hangouts allow you to communicate over the Internet, the enduring telephone network shows no signs of disappearing. Not only do the networks coexist they even seamlessly integrate. You can make a phone call from Skype or dial into a Google Hangouts conference. Established PoW systems may continue to exist and even interoperate with newer PoS systems.

In the coming months and years of blockchain evolution, we expect some of these competing and overlapping systems to integrate. Polkadot,[9] for example, is a platform designed to aggregate and bridge multiple different blockchains and subnetworks. Bitcoin and Ether might trade with each other under a system of shared security (Parker 2019).

The UIs in contemporary DApps are still accessed in a centralized fashion. In one way this is OK in the philosophy of decentralization. The critical parts are decentralized on the blockchain. Ideally the whole application, including the images and visual UI components, are decentralized as well. The blockchain can be used to help secure and distribute those files, not just the programs and tokens. The InterPlanetary File System (IPFS)[10] is one example of a distributed data storage protocol that uses the blockchain to do that. In the future we may see DApps become fully decentralized by using protocols like IPFS to store and serve their files.

In the meantime, the platforms we know will continue to evolve. Proposals for changes to Ethereum can be submitted by anyone and each new proposal is numbered based on its order of submission. EIP-20, the 20th proposal (Vogelstellar and Buterin 2015), became the ERC-20 standard that helped facilitate the ICO boom. With ERC-20, token creators, token exchanges, and Ethereum wallet software could implement a common interface and all these different parties could work together making interoperable products. It is similar to how Sony and Philips released the CD Audio standard so that manufacturers of CDs and CD players, along with music producers, music stores, and consumers, could all use the same type of disc.[11] As of May 2019, the most recent proposal number for Ethereum was 2015.

Vitalik's early article in *Bitcoin Magazine* was exploring "If Bitcoin is to achieve mainstream success…". For centuries we have used money in nearly the same way it was invented—trading pieces of metal for goods and services. The public blockchain is only a few years old and mainstream *awareness* of blockchain continues to grow. We have already seen a number of highs and lows, but true mainstream *success* will be a long-term effort.

---

[9] https://polkadot.network/.

[10] https://ipfs.io/.

[11] Ethereum software, however, is free and open whereas the CD Audio standard was commercially licensed.

References

Bowles N (2017) CryptoKitties, explained … mostly. https://www.nytimes.com/2017/12/28/style/cryptokitties-want-a-blockchain-snuggle.html
Bradbury D (2013) Colored coins paint sophisticated future for Bitcoin. https://www.coindesk.com/colored-coins-paint-sophisticated-future-for-bitcoin
Buterin V (2012) Bitcoin adoption opportunity: teenagers. https://bitcoinmagazine.com/articles/bitcoin-adoption-opportunity-teenager-1330407280/
Buterin V (2013) Mastercoin: a second-generation protocol on the Bitcoin blockchain. https://bitcoinmagazine.com/articles/mastercoin-a-second-generation-protocol-on-the-bitcoin-blockchain-1383603310/
Buterin V (2014a) A next-generation smart contract and decentralized application platform. https://github.com/ethereum/wiki/wiki/White-Paper
Buterin V (2014b) Toward a 12-second block time. https://blog.ethereum.org/2014/07/11/toward-a-12-second-block-time/
CB Insights (2019) Blockchain trends in review. https://www.cbinsights.com/research/report/blockchain-trends-opportunities/
Decker C, Wattenhofer R (2013) Information propagation in the Bitcoin network. https://tik-old.ee.ethz.ch/file//49318d3f56c1d525aabf7fda78b23fc0/P2P2013_041.pdf
ETH News (n.d.) Definition of 'Dapp'. https://www.ethnews.com/glossary/dapp
Hacket R (2016) Can this 22-year-old coder out-bitcoin Bitcoin? http://fortune.com/ethereum-blockchain-vitalik-buterin/
Harford T (2017) The warrior monks who invented banking. https://www.bbc.com/news/business-38499883
Harrington R (2016) How to start your own bank. https://www.huffingtonpost.com/2010/03/19/how-to-start-your-own-ban_n_497261.html
Nakamoto S (2009) Bitcoin: a peer-to-peer electronic cash system. https://bitcoin.org/bitcoin.pdf
National Aeronautics and Space Administration (1971) Spaceborne digital computer systems. https://ntrs.nasa.gov/archive/nasa/casi.ntrs.nasa.gov/19710024203.pdf
Parker E (2019) Ethereum co-founder: 'my biggest disappointment is how toxic this space has become'. https://www.longhash.com/news/ethereum-cofounder-my-biggest-disappointment-is-how-toxic-this-space-has-become
Securities and Exchange Commission (2017) Report of investigation pursuant to Section 21(a) of the Securities Exchange Act of 1934: The DAO. https://www.sec.gov/litigation/investreport/34-81207.pdf
Szabo N (1994) Smart contracts. http://www.fon.hum.uva.nl/rob/Courses/InformationInSpeech/CDROM/Literature/LOTwinterschool2006/szabo.best.vwh.net/smart.contracts.html
Vigna P (2019) Raising money in the Crypto World has gotten a lot harder. https://www.wsj.com/articles/raising-money-in-the-crypto-world-has-gotten-a-lot-harder-11554037201?mod=rsswn
Visa (2019) Visa acceptance for retailers. https://usa.visa.com/run-your-business/small-business-tools/retail.html. Accessed 26 Nov 2019
Vogelstellar F, Buterin V (2015) ERC-20 token standard. https://github.com/ethereum/EIPs/blob/master/EIPS/eip-20.md
Wikipedia Contributors (2019) Turing completeness. https://en.wikipedia.org/wiki/Turing_completeness
Winters T (2016) Decentralized exchange on the Ethereum blockchain. https://www.ethnews.com/decentralized-exchange-on-the-ethereum-blockchain

William Metcalfe is a co-founder of Curvegrid, a blockchain software startup based in Tokyo. Previously, he was the chief technology officer of Gilt Japan after joining the organization in New York City as an early employee. Mr. Metcalfe helped grow Gilt from its first order to become one of the leading ecommerce sites. He graduated from the University of Waterloo with a degree in computer science.

Chapter 6
DEX: A DApp for the Decentralized Marketplace

Chris Dai

It is not an overstatement to say the true value of blockchain technology lies in its ability to use a decentralized model of interaction at the protocol level. This built-in capability is augmenting our Internet, which was built on the ideal of allowing free and unrestricted access to information for all. Instead, the Internet has become the tool for tech giants like Google, Amazon, and Facebook to hold centralized power over its users. Governments have also been able to use this Internet-endowed power to reach to billions of people and manipulate the masses, filter out messages, and limit freedom of speech. Blockchain is the second try at the Internet's idealism, and here we stand in front of this great task. The word "decentralization" seems very utopian, and in the world of a blockchain enthusiast it sounds like a cure for many of the world's problems. But really, what is the value of such decentralization? Is it worth all the effort to break the current centralized organizations and processes into smaller decentralized pieces and micromanage everything at a smaller scale? In our last industrial revolution, value was created through economies of scale. Everyone became a part of a very big machine that output values beyond the sum of the parts. Why are we proposing the opposite now?

This article is based on our final report to the study group "Blockchain and Society 5.0—The Creation of a New Marketplace based on Distributed Consensus" at the Research Institute of Economy, Trade, and Industry (RIETI) .

C. Dai (✉)
Recika Co., Ltd, Tokyo, Japan
e-mail: chris@recika.jp

Leland Capital, Hong Kong, Hong Kong

M. Yano et al. (eds.), *Blockchain and Crypto Currency*,
Economics, Law, and Institutions in Asia Pacific,
https://doi.org/10.1007/978-981-15-3376-1_6

1 Why Are We Getting More Centralized as a Whole?

During the 1970s, the Internet in its infancy was designed as a network of computers in which any two computers could send and receive data to each other even if some nodes on the network failed. This was made possible by the protocols invented by computer scientists like Vinton Cerf. His invention of TCP/IP (Transmission Control Protocol/Internet Protocol) allowed for computers in different small networks to talk to each other (Leiner et al. 2003). This decentralized way of sending information came from the needs of the military in the midst of the Cold War, but later it became widely used by researchers around the world to send files to one another. In 1991, the World Wide Web was introduced, and the Internet's function of sending and receiving data expanded to the creation of a "web" of information that anyone connected could see. However, the TCP/IP protocol or the World Wide Web was designed to send and receive information between devices on the network and did not allow for keeping a shared universal ledger that processed user authentication and recorded transactions. Hence, after the introduction of the World Wide Web, businesses sold products, offered services, distributed entertainment contents, and setup social networking sites, but all the authentication and transaction records had to be stored on the service provider's server. Consumers had to trust the platform to keep their personal data safe and not misuse it. From a business point of view, the scalability of the Internet offered businesses great opportunities. The marginal cost of service was so low and the data that platforms could retrieve and aggregate from consumers was so valuable that the so-called Internet business was highly scalable. From this environment, Internet giants like Google, Amazon, Facebook, and Apple (GAFA) have emerged.

In the current centralized model of the Internet, the power balance between consumers and service providers is severely tilted. Scott Galloway, a professor at the New York University Stern School of Business, where he teaches brand strategy and digital marketing, claims that the growth of GAFA poses a threat to society. He believes the tech giants have succeeded in exerting influence over our attention, our loyalty, and our personal information (Galloway 2017). Many people in the tech industry share the same concerns as Galloway; they fear "centralization" of the Internet in the form of GAFA's increasing control on data and IT infrastructure will discourage innovation.

There are many good reasons behind why companies are becoming more centralized. Coase theorized that companies grow bigger when the frictional cost of trading is high. If the internal transaction cost of a company is lower than transacting with an outside company, then it makes economic sense to internalize that transaction (Coase 1937). Companies that are participants of a market economy are themselves command economies if we consider how they operate internally. A company sets annual or quarterly budgets, goals, and key performance indicators and tries to reach them by allocating resources between departments. With the aid of IT, a company can reach a near real-time tracking and transparent view of the market, and, if it can use the Internet to manage its internal structure and execute on the analysis of market data, then a company managed centrally in a hierarchical way can in fact be very efficient. Information technology helps to lower the frictional cost of trading within the company but does not significantly help the transactions between two unknown parties. Because the frictional cost between two unknown parties is a trust issue, we have traditionally relied on a third party to witness, record, and carry out the transaction. By lowering the external transaction cost, we hope companies do not have to get bigger and bigger to achieve efficiency.

With the use of blockchain, we are now able to run a marketplace in a decentralized way to exchange data and value. By lowering the frictional cost of transaction between unknown parties, we can finally make decentralization cost effective and take away control of the marketplace from central authorities.

2 Tokenization at Different Layers of Blockchain

Blockchain is sometimes also called the "chain of values". Most of the assets that represent value can be represented and owned on the blockchain in the form of "tokens". Because tokens are issued on different layers of the blockchain, we first need to understand the values that tokens represent at each layer of the blockchain. There are three layers of blockchain that can issue tokens or "tokenize" (see Fig. 1).

2.1 Crypto Asset Token and Its Value

Crypto asset tokens can represent anything from a movie ticket to a gallon of oil or one hour someone's donated time. Because these tokens actually represent assets or values in the physical world, tokenization at this layer is very similar to securitization in the financial world where companies can securitize a real asset or some form of rights for the objective of trading.

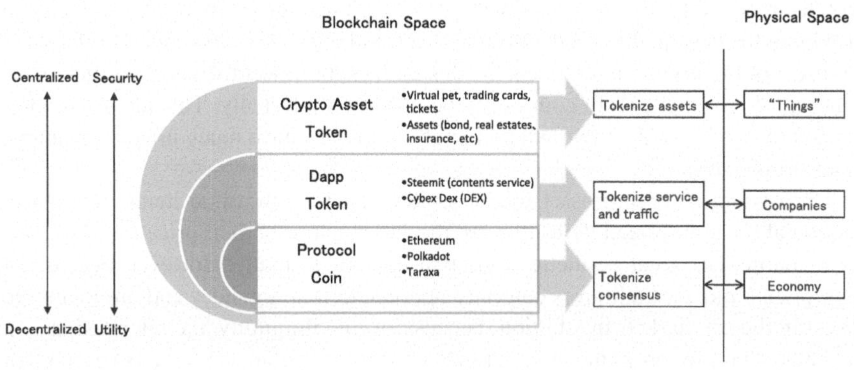

Fig. 1 Tokenization at different layers of blockchain

The issuing of these tokens requires a central entity to maintain the reserves of the actual assets, issue the representing tokens on the blockchain, and guarantee that anyone holding the token can redeem the underlying asset anytime. Blockchain allows for easy issuing of crypto asset tokens and there are many common standards offered by blockchain protocols such as Ethereum, EOS, and so on. The benefit of issuing crypto asset tokens is the ability to create a digital public voucher that cannot be faked and represents some form of rights in regard to the underlying real asset. In addition, the issuing cost for crypto asset tokens is low because no third party or intermediary is needed. The cost only reflects the cost of keeping a record in the public ledger, which is very low. Furthermore, the token or digital voucher itself can contain logic that will be automatically executed and thereby lowers the management cost of the token. For example, if a crypto asset token represents an event ticket, it can be programmed so that after a certain date (e.g., the event date) the token will delete itself. Requirements for approval from multiple parties can also be incorporated (e.g., to transfer the ticket to another person or entity), thus implementing rules for governance.

2.2 Economic Benefit of Tokenization

The lower issuing cost of crypto asset tokens allows many assets that are non-standard, of low value, or illiquid to be "securitized", thereby creating a new market-place for products and services. For example, farmers can issue tokens representing their livestock to collateralize a micro financing loan issued on blockchain. A sports trainer can issue tokens for professional contact time to provide more accurate pricing of services and better scheduling. A restaurant can issue tokens for seats, while a garment manufacturer in China can issue tokens to represent its production capacity of T-shirts so that it will not be affected by the high/low season cycle of manufacturing. The tokenization of various resources in our economy allows values that are internally recognized within a company or organization to be externally valued along with the risk and return associated with it. As such, resource producers can focus on providing the best quality products or services and worry less about market risks and the price of the crypto asset token. To this end, crypto asset tokens allow the externalizing of risk that before could only be absorbed internally. This allows smaller players to survive in a system where larger companies have much bigger advantage in absorbing risks.

The issuing of crypto asset tokens is not just for low-value items but is also beneficial for high-priced items that are illiquid because of their price tag. Artwork, for example, has great aesthetic value that appeals to many. However, because of high prices, most art admirers can only appreciate it at a gallery and are unable to invest in the art market. In addition, because of this illiquidity, the intermediary on the value chain for art items (e.g., art galleries) usually charge a large percentage of the fee, squeezing the artist and the collector. Tokenizing artwork can allow partial ownership of the art, so that anyone can achieve partial ownership of an artwork.

Furthermore, artists can issue crypto asset tokens for their artwork much like crowd funding, providing the buyer with public proof of ownership and better opportunity to resale, while taking away the cost of the intermediary and allowing for higher liquidity.

2.3 Enabling Truly Effective and Fair Exchange

A new type of marketplace called a decentralized exchange (DEX) is particularly useful because it offers secure peer-to-peer exchange of crypto asset tokens. DEXs offer the perfect marketplace for trading of crypto asset tokens between token holders. A centralized marketplace is a black box that relies on all the participating parties to trust the marketplace to be efficient and fair. However, this is not always the case. FX trading platforms in Japan make profit based on the spread between the buy and sell prices instead of the transaction fee. This means the market operator is also participating as a trading counter party that has the advantage of knowing all the ask and bid prices and can react to the market before all the players. This unfair advantage brings the central exchange operator continuous trading profits. A decentralized exchange on the other hand only has two parties involved; that is, the buyer and the seller. The market itself is only a set of program instructions that makes sure that when a deal is matched between the buyer and seller, no one can back out after both parties have signed. The transaction itself is recorded on the blockchain, so it is easily traced. Instead of trusting a third party to store all the transaction data, it is safer and better to save it on the blockchain so no one can change it later (immutability) and everyone can check it to prove the legitimacy of the trading (transparency) .

By allowing peer-to-peer trading, liquidity is also added to the market where the asset may not have had any physical trading or the legitimacy of ownership was difficult to prove online. In the case of artwork, the number of central exchanges (i.e., auction houses) is limited and only a small group of rich customers/investors are able to participate in the market. These traits make the market very illiquid. However, if artwork tokens are issued in a decentralized exchange, each token can represent partial ownership of the artwork and people who are interested in art can buy and sell tokens and profit from it even if they do not have the money to buy a whole piece of artwork. Because the decentralized exchange is run on automated computer codes, its fee is much lower that of an auction house, and thus can attract more buy and sell transactions. Allowing more players and more transactions in this marketplace allows for liquidity and liquidity creates value. In essence, the crypto asset token value is derived from the value of its underlying asset, plus the liquidity premium generated from the lowering of transaction costs.

2.4 Decentralized Application Tokens and Their Value

As explained in previous chapters, decentralized applications, or DApps, interact with the blockchain through smart contracts. These applications can also issue their own tokens and these tokens can be traded together with the crypto asset tokens. This is an interesting yet confusing scheme, so it is worth explaining through an example. Cybex is a decentralized exchange DApp that hosts a peer-to-peer marketplace for tokens to be exchanged. Cybex also issues its own token (CYB), which can be used in the Cybex marketplace to pay fees to issue new types of tokens, staking to borrow crypto asset tokens for trading, voting for block producers, and paying for transaction fees for trades in the Cybex marketplace. If the value of a crypto asset token represents the value of the underlying asset + liquidity premium, what is the value of a token issued by a DApp?

First, a DApp token is used as a voucher to receive service in the DApp. Service includes issuing new crypto asset tokens and trading tokens. Because the number of DApp tokens in the system is usually fixed, as more people use the Cybex marketplace to exchange tokens, the demand for CYB increases, and the price of CYB goes up. Hence, the value or price of CYB used as a service voucher depends on the transaction volume and the user traffic on the system.

Second, CYB functions like a share because the token gives the holder voting rights; the holder may have the opportunity to vote on whether additional functions can be implemented in the system, whether a new consensus algorithm needs to be implemented, or which node gets to be the block-producing node, and so on. The holder of CYB is also a shareholder of Cybex in the sense that they have the right to governance of the system and to influence how the ecosystem is run. Ideally, a DApp in its fully decentralized and open-source form will not need a company structure to support it. Also, the ownership of the ecosystem is shared by the participants/token owners. Therefore, it does not make sense to issue equity to its investors because the shares will represent nothing.

A DApp token also represents the shareholding value of the DApp ecosystem. The clear difference from the current company structure is that a DApp native token can be used both as a voucher to the service as well as a shareholding right, but a company like Google will not allow its investors to pay service fees with Google shares. Good or bad, blockchain enables unrelated types of transactions to be encapsulated in a single type of asset with multiple dimensions of value, which increases the difficulty of regulation but allows innovation and value creation through breaking the walls between different business segments. We will see this type of value creation in blockchain in all its layers again and again.

It is also important to note that although tokens created in the purely decentralized application can represent both the service voucher and ownership of the ecosystem or cash flow, there are very few purely decentralized applications in the world. Most DApps created in the near future will be somewhat centralized. Binance token, for example, is built on the trust of the Binance company (one of the largest crypto exchanges in the world) and not blockchain. Therefore, we may need to evaluate the actual value of DApp tokens on a case by case basis, depending on the level of decentralization and how tokens are used in the DApp.

2.5 *Protocol Layer Coin and Its Value*

If we equate the crypto asset token value to representing things in the physical world, and Dapp tokens to value as shares of companies, then what is the value of protocol layer tokens or "coin" as most people call them in the blockchain community? First, the blockchain protocol layer is where the ledger (the public record) and the consensus algorithm (rules about who writes to the ledger) are defined. Within the blockchain network, mining nodes and full nodes provide the infrastructure of the public blockchain that maintains correct recording of transactions to the blockchain and prevents attacks to the blockchain. The function of the protocol in the blockchain world is similar to the function of the constitution and legal system of a nation or economy in the physical world. The codes that run on all nodes in a blockchain are similar to the set of rules we create in our physical world in the form of law. Protocol usage is not free because incentives have to be given to individuals to share their resources as part of the infrastructure. Therefore, every transaction will pay a transaction fee to record a transaction to the ledger. This is similar to tax levied on individuals and companies in the physical world. Coins within the protocol are usually used to pay for transaction fees using the protocol.

What is the value of the coin? This is like asking the value of the US dollar. Many argue that the US dollar is backed by the US Government and therefore has value, but coins issued on blockchain are not backed by anyone and therefore should have no value. Interestingly, on every single US dollar bill, there is one sentence: "IN GOD WE TRUST" (Department of the Treasury website 2011). In some way, it would be more appropriate to say "in the US Government we trust" or "in the Federal Reserve we trust." This tells us that the value of the US dollar relies more on the individual faith in a collective imagination than on a central authority. Trust of money in a democracy and a market economy comes from the consensus of every member of the society that he or she agrees to exchange value to that money at any time. This trust is a collective trust, and this trust is realized on the blockchain using coins and tokens. In essence, coin is a medium of exchange but also represents the trust of the participants in the ecosystem.

Unlike the real world, where individuals may not be able to choose their country or economy, choosing a blockchain is much easier and simply requires the purchase of tokens or coins to transact with others. This kind of liquidity allows for competition between blockchain protocols, and, ultimately, should lead to the improvement of blockchain protocol. At the protocol layer, there should be no real owner of the protocol because it is an infrastructure. Protocol is more decentralized than the DApp, which limits the development team's monetization method to mainly token sale.

3 What Is a DEX?

So far, we have explained how blockchain tokens can be used to represent and record value data and build new business models that open up that data to all participants in the system. However, if only token issuing on the blockchain uses the decentralized model while exchange of tokens is done centrally, then the full potential of the blockchain decentralized model cannot be achieved.

When Adam Smith proposed the concept of the invisible hand, he still envisioned the marketplace itself to be run by a central entity (Smith 1776). Today we see many marketplaces in the world: marketplaces for consumer products like Amazon or securities markets like the New York Stock Exchange or the Tokyo Stock Exchange, and commodity exchange markets like the Chicago Mercantile Exchange, and so on. These marketplaces together create the backbone of our market economy, channeling and optimizing the flow of money to the right industry and assets. However, most of these exchanges are not as efficient as we might think. There are many intermediaries between the buyer and seller and some transactions have very complicated and manual settlement processes that take many days to clear. With blockchain, a new type of Dapp[1] called "DEX" (as shorthand for "decentralized exchange") is about to change the way we trade with each other.

A decentralized exchange on the blockchain has the following characteristics:

- Allows peer-to-peer exchange of token/crypto assets without an intermediary party.
- Each participant controls his/her own asset (private key).
- All transactions are written on the blockchain and are transparent for the public to see.
- All transactions after confirmation are immutable.

3.1 Key Technical Core of a DEX

In the previous section, we argued for the benefit of DEX and considered the types of asset that can be traded on a DEX. It is also worthwhile to take a closer look at the technical features of a DEX and how it is implemented. The core of a DEX is a feature called "atomic swap", which is code on the blockchain that allows two parties to exchange tokens/crypto assets without involving an intermediary party, and avoids one party defaulting on the transaction, which would damage the counter party. In a DEX, unlike a centralized exchange, participants manage their own crypto assets in their own wallet. When there is an exchange between two parties, the exchange occurs directly between the two wallets instead of going through a trusted third party. This direct exchange process is called atomic swap. There are many ways to implement atomic swap and Fig. 2 shows the method proposed by Charlie Lee, the founder of Litecoin.

[1] An application run by many users on a decentralized network with trustless protocols. https://en.wikipedia.org/wiki/Decentralized_application.

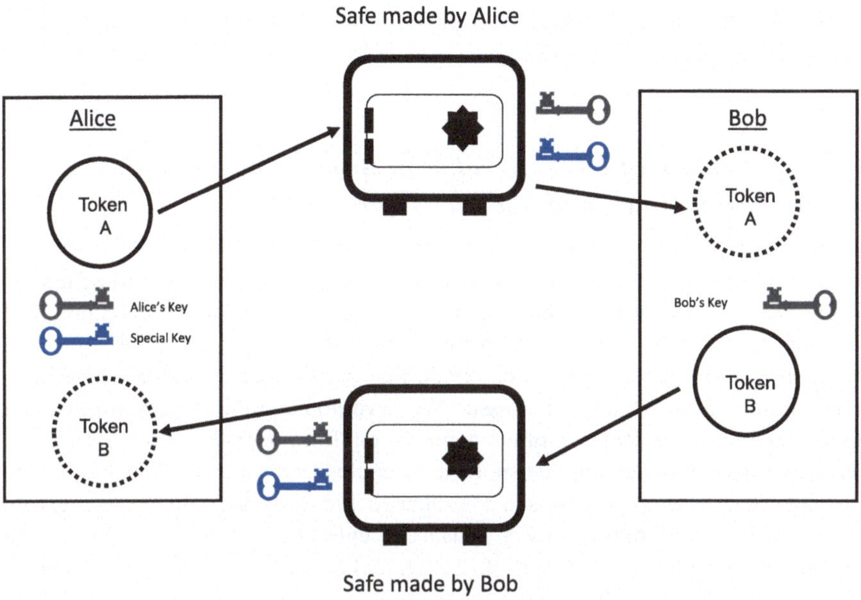

Fig. 2 An example of atomic swap

Figure 2 shows a case with two participants, Alice and Bob, who want to swap tokens on two different blockchains with each other. Alice holds token A of blockchain A and Bob holds token B of blockchain B. First, Alice and Bob agree on an exchange rate of 1 A token for 1 B token. Negotiation of the exchange price occurs on a buy/sell board or a chat board. After the exchange rate is agreed, Alice creates a digital safe on chain A that can be opened by Bob's key and a special key created by Alice and unknown to Bob. Alice puts 1 A token in the safe and sends safe information to Bob, sharing the specifications of the lock for the special key without sharing the key. Bob then also creates a digital safe on chain B and puts 1 B token in the safe. Bob's safe can only be opened by Alice's key and the special key used together, but when the special key is used by Alice to open the safe on chain B, the special key will be revealed to Bob. Similarly, Bob uses his own key and the revealed special key to open the safe box on chain A and the transaction is completed. The locks on both safe boxes have a time limit, and if Alice does not open the safe box on chain B, or Bob does not create the safe box on chain B and send the information to Alice, then the tokens in the safe will be returned to the original owners without causing loss to either party. In this case, after Alice opens the safe on chain B, there is no turning back and the transaction will be carried out. This is why the process is called "atomic swap", because it follows the original concept that the atom is not divisible, and this process is designed so that transaction between two chains can be whole and not divisible after both parties commit. Atomic swap provides predictable and transparent exchange of tokens on different blockchains on the basis of code and not based on the trust of a third party. In the next section, we examine its implications and impact through actual cases.

3.2 Implication of DEX: Revolution Brought by the Ability to Issue, Trade, and Record Crypto Assets

While the merit of the atomic swap is very clear for trading crypto assets, the function of the DEX reaches far beyond that of an exchange. Compared to a centralized exchange, which can only be used for exchange of crypto assets, a DEX can use its chain to issue new crypto assets, trade that crypto asset, and record business transactions related to the crypto asset. We have no centralized platform that can do all three together. Binance offers a central platform to trade crypto assets, but, because it is centralized and does not use blockchain to run its exchange, it has to manually issue new crypto assets in its exchange. Similarly, a DApp that uses crypto assets cannot record transactions on Binance's central trading platform. What is the benefit of doing all three processes of issuing, trading, and recording transactions on a single blockchain? If all activities related to a single crypto asset are recorded on the same blockchain, then users and investors can get full view of usage/transaction and transaction records of the issuing party. This creates more transparency and adds credibility to the crypto assets. With transparency around transaction data, a DEX can truly become an ecosystem to host services and allow liquidity to crypto assets backed with goods and services.

The value of a DEX is clearly demonstrated in RECIKA's[2] consumer data marketplace project that aims to democratize the trading of consumer purchasing data. By using a DEX as the core system, RECIKA allows individuals to upload the scan of their purchasing receipts to receive tokens while businesses that want to access uploaded consumer data can pay tokens to retrieve the data. In the current business model, consumer purchasing data are stored in retailers' databases but retailers are not incentivized to share this data. It is difficult for smaller manufacturers and startups to access such consumer purchasing data. By acknowledging consumers' ownership rights to their consumption data and attaining their consent to share that data, such data can be circulated between consumers, retailers, and manufacturers. All the data transactions are recorded on the DEX blockchain to allow for transparency in the system. Any participant can check how much data is being uploaded and how much data is exchanged. In addition, manufacturers can issue their own point reward system by issuing their own tokens to any consumer that has uploaded a receipt containing the manufacturer's product. Issued points (tokens) of all the manufacturers can also be traded on the DEX, so consumers can convert points from different manufacturers to the desired manufacturer when needed. All this can be achieved in the centralized system, but generally the consumer and/or manufacturer do not trust their data and points to an intermediary. Rather than trusting a third party

[2]For more information on RECIKA, please visit www.recika.jp.

that may leak consumers' privacy data or abuse the power they hold over consumers and manufacturers, a decentralized ecosystem will receive more support from the different parties involved.

Another use case built on top of DEX is the issuing of tickets. A DEX allows for applications to issue fungible[3] and non-fungible[4] tokens and peer-to-peer transfer and trade of those tokens. These functions are very convenient for event organizers and ticket issuers. In Japan, most event tickets are not digitized and many small to medium-sized event organizers still use fax to confirm reservations. The big ticket platforms charge a significant fee that small to medium-sized companies cannot afford. By issuing tickets as tokens on the DEX chain, the cost of issuing tickets is lowered but it also allows for a secondary market where trading of the tickets is possible, and the legitimacy of the ticket is verifiable. The ticket token issued on the blockchain becomes the digital identification that attendees of the event can show at the event reception counter.

3.3 Challenges for DEX

While the trading of data and tickets on DEX may seem benign to financial regulatory bodies, trading of crypto currencies and other financial securities on a peer-to-peer basis poses serious concerns in the area of money laundering and the funding of crime and terrorism. This concern is not just for DEX but for crypto currency as a whole. Because of the lack of central authentication, many DEXs do not require "know your customer" (KYC) to function and do not have a clear entity of responsibility for liaising with government regulatory bodies. For DEX to be used more widely, it is true that functions such as KYC and accountability need to be built into the code, which may result in more centralized operation of a DEX. DEX also offers the opportunity for regulatory agencies and society as a whole to monitor for suspicious transactions and operations in a drastically different paradigm. Blockchain offers an ocean of global financial transaction data that is transparent to all. It allows anyone to retrieve and analyze data, which is very difficult to achieve in the current financial industry where every bank hides transactions in highly secure servers. Utilizing AI technology with this big data allows regulation technology to be developed that can find, monitor, and trace illicit activity on the blockchain with very high efficiency.

Aside from the regulatory challenges, the current DEX user base is not growing fast despite its obvious benefits because of the low performance of the underlying blockchain technology. The transaction speed of a centralized exchange is 100× or 1000× that of the current best performing DEX, giving the user a much better

[3]Fungibility is the property of a good or a commodity that has individual units that are essentially interchangeable.

[4]A non-fungible token (NFT) is a special type of cryptographic token that represents something unique; thus, NFTs are not interchangeable. This is in contrast to crypto currencies like Bitcoin, and many network or utility tokens that are fungible in nature.

experience. There is much work to be done to solve the scalability issue of blockchain and hopefully it will bring the proliferation of DEX.

Ultimately, our biggest challenge is ourselves. We are too comfortable with relying on centralized authority to manage what is most valuable and dearest to us, may it be our personal data or asset possessions. In this process, we are in danger of losing not only our privacy but also being taken advantage of by central authorities that are able to use our data to influence our behaviors. Blockchain-enabled DEX puts everyone standing at the crossroad again, providing us with the option to choose and to be in control once more.

References

Coase R (1937) The nature of the firm. Economica 4:386–405

Department of the Treasury website (2011). https://www.treasury.gov/about/education/Pages/in-god-we-trust.aspx

Galloway S (2017) *The four: The hidden DNA of Amazon, Apple, Facebook, and Google*. Amazon Service International

Leiner BM, Cerf VG, Clark DD, Kahn RE, Kleinrock L, Lynch DC, Postel J, Roberts LG, Wolff S (2003) A brief history of Internet

Smith A (1776) The wealth of nations

Chris Dai is the CEO and co-founder of Leland Capital, Recika Co., Ltd., and CEO of LongHash Japan. He has a broad range of business management and investment experience. He was formerly the COO/CIO of Yixing SCM (an international logistics provider), a consultant at Accenture, and a co-founder of multiple ventures. Starting in 2013, Mr. Dai was one of the early investors in Bitcoin and Ethereum. To promote the understanding of blockchain's true value, he joined the Research Institute of Economy, Trade and Industry's blockchain research team. He received a B.S. in management science and engineering from Stanford University in 2004.

Chapter 7
Blockchain Business and Its Regulation

Makoto Yano, Chris Dai, Kenichi Masuda and Yoshio Kishimoto

As the blockchain industry becomes larger, a new decentralized financial ecosystem is now developing. New financial instruments, represented by terms like tokens, coins, and ICOs are introduced to finance projects on blockchain. Blockchain is a technology that makes it possible to assign ownership of each piece of data to individuals who create that piece. As Pu and Yano (2020) points out, that may be the first step towards creating a high quality market.[1] At the same time, like a lock, blockchain is merely a technology that is designed to protect a type of property. Such a technology is of no use unless the society agrees a proper set of rules concerning

[1] See Yano (2019) for details on market quality.

The original version of this chapter is written as a part of our final report to the study group "Blockchain and Society 5.0—The Creation of a New Marketplace based on Distributed Consensus" at the Research Institute of Economy, Trade, and Industry (RIETI). The authors are grateful to all the participant in the study group. The first author gratefully acknowledges the financial support of a Grant-in-Aid for Scientific Research (A) (#16H02015) from the Japan Society for the Promotion of Science.

M. Yano (✉)
Research Institute of Economy, Trade and Industry (RIETI), Tokyo, Japan
e-mail: yano-makoto@rieti.go.jp

C. Dai
Recika Co., Ltd, Tokyo, Japan
e-mail: chris@recika.jp

K. Masuda
Anderson Mori & Tomotsune, Tokyo, Japan

Y. Kishimoto
Ministry of Economy, Trade and Industry, Tokyo, Japan

M. Yano et al. (eds.), *Blockchain and Crypto Currency*,
Economics, Law, and Institutions in Asia Pacific,
https://doi.org/10.1007/978-981-15-3376-1_7

how to prevent the abuse of the technology, what should be protected and how to protect it. The present study is concerned with this issue.

Many countries are now studying how to create a new financial ecosystem in which a high quality market can be supported for blockchain products. The USA is now regulating it under the Securities Act whereas Japan is applying the Money Settlement Act and the Financial Instruments and Exchange Act. In this chapter, without going into country-specific regulatory issues, we investigate how society may deal with the new decentralized financial ecosystem from a regulatory viewpoint to create a macroeconomy with high quality markets.

To design a desirable financial system for the blockchain industry, we should examine blockchain applications from the following four perspectives.

1. Comparison between decentralized and conventional financial devices.
2. Different fundraising methods for blockchain projects.
3. Desirable regulations for current blockchain applications.
4. Regulation and self-regulation of the future blockchain industry.

Before starting our discussion, it is worth emphasizing that experts regard a completely decentralized blockchain to be ideal. In such a blockchain, although someone has central control in the developmental stage, no single entity is legally charged with responsibility to maintain and improve a blockchain (although there are organizations such as the Ethereum foundation that voluntarily maintain and improve different blockchains). Maintenance and improvement are left to development community members (most likely computer specialists), who make voluntary contributions. This clearly differs from ordinary businesses, which have owners, and even the way companies are set up.

As discussed in Chapter 1, there are two types of blockchain applications: currencies and business applications. It is not desirable to treat the two types of applications under a single regulation. In what follows, we discuss the design of regulations on blockchain applications for each of these types.

In Sect. 1 of this chapter, we discuss regulations on blockchains for currency purposes, such as Bitcoin and Bitcoin Cash. To understand why currency blockchains should be treated separately from those for business projects, it is important first to understand the difference between money and standard businesses and how they are treated in a conventional financial ecosystem. We will then cover regulations on currency blockchain.

In Sect. 2, we discuss the current state of fundraising for blockchain businesses. ICOs are often designed as a way of bypassing securities regulations; issuers have argued coins and tokens do not fall under the regulatory definition of securities. As blockchain businesses expand, however, various ICOs are regarded as securities offerings in more and more countries. To adjust to this atmosphere, some issuers of blockchain tokens have started to issue tokens more in line with securities regulations. These offerings are referred to as security token offerings (STOs).

In Sect. 3, we discuss issues in designing regulations on fundraising for blockchain businesses from the viewpoint of information disclosure. We discuss the difficulties of continuous information disclosure after the project is completed and opened to the general public.

In the long run, it may be desirable to develop a system of financial regulations and compliances that is more in line with the decentralized features of blockchain businesses. In Sect. 4, we discuss regulatory issues in a future decentralized financial ecosystem after blockchain establishes its position in the real-world economy.

1 Risky and Risk-Free Decentralized Assets

At the moment, there is no general consensus in the world on how to regulate fundraisings by blockchain businesses. The ways in which regulations are designed in many countries do not perfectly match blockchain technology. Regulators are still struggling to decide how they should deal with fundraisings for blockchain projects.

The biggest cause for this situation probably stems from the fact that the term "virtual currency" is used in a broad manner. Fundraisings for blockchain projects are associated with various instruments: Tokens, coins, and currencies. What they are is, however, very unclear.

To clarify various concepts associated with blockchain, it may be desirable to take an economic approach. From the economic viewpoint, assets can be classified into two types: risky and riskfree. To set a benchmark for our discussion, it is important to understand their difference in a simple stylized framework.

For that purpose, consider two states of nature: 1 and 2. Which of the two states of nature is realized is not known for sure, but the probabilities with which they are realized are known. In Fig. 1, the returns to a project for the cases in which states 1 and 2 are realized are measured along the horizontal and vertical axes, respectively.

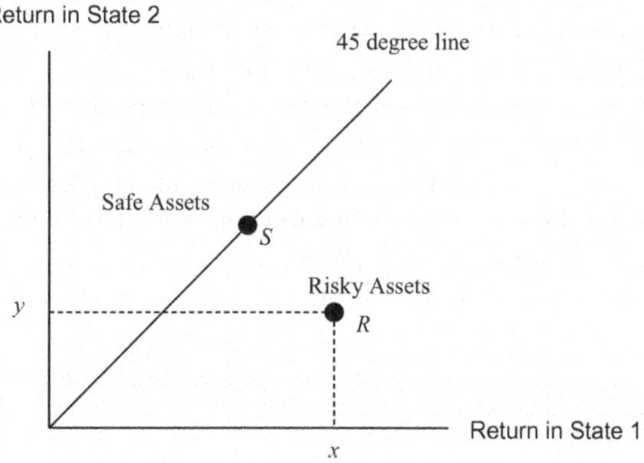

Fig. 1 Risky assets and safe assets

In Fig. 1, the return to a risk-free asset can be indicated by a point on the 45-degree line; when such a point implies that the return in one state of nature is equal to that in the other state of nature, the underlying project is said to be risk free. In contrast, the return to a risky asset can be indicated by a point off the 45-degree line. If the return at point (x, y) implies that it is equal to x in state 1 whereas it is equal to y in state 2. The underlying project in this case is said to be risky.

Stocks and bonds issued by companies are thought of as risky assets, the values of which tend to fluctuate. Money is regarded as a risk-free asset in the world without inflation and deflation. It is generally agreed that risky assets and risk-free asset s should be regulated separately because the nature of underlying risk differs between risky and risk-free assets.

Blockchain projects can also be classified into two types. Risk-free projects aim to create risk-free assets such as Bitcoin, Ethereum (the base currency for Ethereum), and IOTA. Although Bitcoin and Ethereum are currently subject to large risks, the nature of the risks are similar to those associated with international currencies; for that reason, they may be classified as risk-free assets. The other type aims to create various applications for online services like those provided by DApps.

1.1 Roles on Securities Markets

Traditionally, as is noted above, fundraisings for creating risk-free and risky assets are regulated under completely separate systems. To understand this separation, it is desirable to start with how businesses are started and developed into established entities.

It is a prerequisite for business investment to evaluate the business. At an early stage of an enterprise, it is not economical for market participants to gather necessary information on business prospects. In that case, a company has to rely on bank loans and its own funds. Once the business grows, it becomes economical for market participants to invest in a company after evaluating business performance. Two types of markets exist for companies at such a stage to raise funds: venture capital markets and initial public offering (IPO) markets.

In a venture capital market, companies that are not yet very established raise funds from professional investors called venture capitalists, who are specialized in investing companies at early stages. In an IPO market, companies that are well established sell their stocks to open markets in which ordinary investors, with less accurate information, participate.

1.2 Securities Regulations: From Caveat Emptor to Caveat Venditor

When the Great Depression started in 1929, many people found that it was caused by shady operations in the financial industry during the 1920s (Seligman 1982). To fix these problems, President Roosevelt established the Securities Act of 1933 and the Securities Exchange Act of 1934. The US Securities and Exchange Commission (SEC), established under the 1934 Act, adopted Rule 10b-5, which stipulated that it is illegal "for any person

(a) To employ any device, scheme, or artifice to defraud,
(b) To make any untrue statement of a material fact or to omit a material fact necessary in order to make the statements made, in the light of the circumstances under which they were made, not misleading, or
(c) To engage in any fact, practice, or course of business which operates or would operate as a fraud or deceit upon any person, in connection with the purchase or sale of any security."

From an economic viewpoint, it is desirable to maintain symmetric information between sellers and buyers; in other words, they should make their respective decisions based on common information. In general, the seller has an informational advantage with respect to an object to be traded, although in many cases the informational disparity can easily be fixed if sufficient diligence is exercised before the transaction. In certain cases, however, fixing is difficult or highly costly. This is particularly so in the case of securities transactions, in which a large informational advantage is held by the issuer of a security and insiders of a company of which the securities are on open market. The Securities Act and the Securities Exchange Act are intended to maintain informational parity in the securities market.

These Acts represent a landmark in securities regulations shifting from the long traditional rule of *caveat emptor* (let the buyer beware) to *caveat venditor* (let the seller beware). Since the eighteenth century, in the USA, it had been held that "[t]he law requires the purchaser in all cases to use the utmost diligence in the investigation of the right, title and quality of the thing to be purchased, and if he does not, then in the absence of positive fraud on the part of the vendor, he must take the goods he finds them with all faults."[2]

This conventional rule has been shifted by the Securities Act and the Securities Exchange Act, which regulates IPOs and insider trade in the stock market. Securities issuers are, as we discuss in detail in Sect. 3, required to disclose information relevant for ordinary investors in stock markets to allow them to make informed decisions.

An exception to this rule can be found in venture capital investment (private placement), in which securities are sold not in an open market but to a small number of chosen investors. Although, even in private placements, securities issuers are subject to the Securities Act, they are not required to register their securities with

[2]For old cases on *caveat emptor*, see Chandelor v. Lopus, 79 Eng. Rep. 3 (1603). Also see Lowenthal (1891).

the SEC, which is rather costly. In the case of private placements, investors are professional experts rather than ordinary investors in stock markets, in which case they can be expected to be capable of obtaining necessary information on investment target by exercising due diligence.

1.3 Money and Tokens

In ICOs (or fundraising for blockchain projects), money is often provided in exchange for a certificate called a token or a coin rather than a security. In general, coins refer to the base currency in blockchain systems. Examples are Bitcoin and Ethereum. Tokens are digital currencies that can be issued and distributed using smart contracts and Dapps on blockchains. In many cases, however, tokens and coins are not clearly distinguished.

Traditionally, token is a synonym for ticket; for example, a ticket for New York Subway used to be called a token, which was a coin-shaped metal piece. Tokens are also used in many amusement arcades.

Within a subway system or within an amusement arcade, tokens are risk-free assets. If the subway toll is 25 cents, a quarter can be used instead of a token that is sold for 25 cents. In other words, tokens and money are much the same within the subway.

In several respects, it makes good sense that investment certificates for ICOs are called tokens, instead of securities. First, blockchain projects are based on decentralization, in which sense they are completely different from centrally managed conventional enterprises in their nature. Second, it is highly costly to issue a security for fundraisers to comply with securities regulations.

1.3.1 Money and Securities Regulations

Money is the most common risk-free asset. The conventional currency system was explained in detail in Chapter 4. In nineteenth century United States, commercial banks issued banknotes that promised conversion with government-issued gold coins or government bonds and were circulated as currency. However, once a recession occurred, many individual commercial banks failed to repay the banknotes that they issued by whatever the banknotes were set to be convertible, which caused many bank runs.

To overcome this problem, the central banking system was created in 1913. The Federal Reserve Bank, established by law, started to issue dollar bills, which gradually replaced private banknotes by the 1930s. In 1933, during the Great Depression, the Federal Deposit Insurance Corporation was established, which provided insurance to deposits held by member banks. At the same time, the gold standard was abolished, whereby the fiat money system was adopted.

Risk-free assets such as currencies have not been regarded as securities and been placed outside of securities regulations. Instead, currencies are regulated by separate regulations with a different purpose. As discussed in Chapter 4, regulations on currencies aim to give and maintain trust in what the central authority circulates as a currency. In the case of a virtual currency, in contrast, trust is created by an algorithm without any involvement of the central authority. After it is put into use, a virtual currency protocol is improved and maintained on a voluntary basis by a community of software engineers.

The closer to money the service provided by a blockchain, the less likely fundraisings for the blockchain are to be subject to securities regulations. In a recent position paper, the SEC announced that if blockchain is more "immediately be used to make payments in a wide variety of contexts, or acts as a substitute for real (or fiat) currency," fundraisings for the blockchain are less likely to be regarded as a security issue. Moreover, if it is more likely that "essential tasks for development, improvement (or enhancement), operation, or promotion of the network are expected to be performed by an unaffiliated, dispersed community of network users (commonly known as a "decentralized" network)," fundraisings are less likely to be subject to securities regulations (Securities and Exchange Commission 2019a). This view reflects the unique feature of public network building to which many people contribute to without any payment for their services.

1.3.2 Token as a Ticket Under Securities Regulations

Conventional tickets, in particular for sporting events and concerts, are often traded in a secondary market. In some cases, tickets that are purchased purely for the purpose of attending an event will be sold in a secondary market if, for some reason or another, it becomes impossible for the ticket owner. In other cases, tickets are bought for scalping; that is, not for attending an event but for reselling them to those who want to attend the event at a higher price. Even if a ticket is purchased for attending an event, it is a risky asset, because it is always possible that circumstances may prevent attendance. If tickets are purchased purely for reselling, it is a speculation, in which case tickets are undoubtedly a risky asset. Thus, tickets are risky assets. However, in many countries, tickets are treated outside of securities regulations.

Because tickets are risky assets, a question has been raised as to whether tickets are subject to the securities law. For the moment, a ticket is thought of as "a commodity purchased for use or consumption" and is placed outside of the securities regulations. The SEC does not object to this interpretation.

Under the US securities regulations, investment contracts are regarded as securities. In 1946, the US Supreme Court defined an investment contract as a transaction or scheme that "involves [1] an investment of money [2] in a common enterprise [3] with profits to come solely from the efforts of others"; this standard for investment contracts is referred to as the *Howey* test.[3]

---

[3]"Securities and Exchange Commission v. W. J. Howey Co.," 328 U.S. 293 (1946).

It is generally considered that tickets do not pass this test and are not regarded as securities. That is, although a ticket purchase is an investment of money, it is not regarded as an investment in a common enterprise. This is because "the purchasers of tickets have no financial relationship with each other and that each purchaser's fortune relates to his or her sale of a ticket belonging solely to that purchaser."[4]

Moreover, investments that are not for profit are not considered as investment contracts. For example, according to the US Supreme Court, a contract in which you pay money only for the purpose of using a particular service with a promise that the money will be repaid when you no longer need that service is not regarded as a security.[5]

2 ICO

As noted above, many different functions are provided by what are called virtual currencies. Certain virtual currencies provide monetary function, like Bitcoin. Others function like securities of which the returns are linked with business performances. For example, one of the virtual currency exchanges, Binance, issued a virtual currency called BNB in 2017. In addition to discounted fees for trading in BNB, Binance promises buybacks of BNB tokens by spending 20% of Binance's annual profits.

2.1 Utility Tokens

During the early days of ICO funding, investments were concentrated on protocol projects that created the base of blockchain. At the stage of raising funds, it was common for a software developer to issue on Ethereum what was called an IOU token, which promised to be exchanged for a base currency coin to be created by the new blockchain project. When investors invested in IOU (monetary bond) tokens, money was sent in Ethereum (ETH) or Bitcoin (BTC) into the smart contract that the fundraiser had created on Ethereum in advance. The smart contract automatically recorded both the payment amount and the recipient's account (address) on Ethereum blockchain as well as the receipt of IOU tokens. Therefore, if the real value of the token was unclear for investors, at least the receipt of tokens was guaranteed.

The first problem in this process is that an IOU token may be regarded as a security. Once a particular protocol's base currency is in use, the IOU tokens will be exchanged for base currency coins. In some countries, those base currency coins may be recognized as securities, in which case they would become subject to securities regulations. In fear of being put under securities regulations, most ICO projects

[4]See Gonson (2003) and the SEC's response to the letter (Securities and Exchange Commission 2003).

[5]"United Housing Foundation, Inc. v. Foreman," 421 U.S. 837 (1975).

(especially protocol development projects) argued that their coins were utility tokens. According to them, in other words, they were like tickets to use the services created by the project that the issuer was to create.

If utility tokens are tickets purely to be used to receive the services of a project, they are not securities, and, as a result, placed under regulations that are looser than securities regulations. It is generally thought that fundraising by means of a utility token is appropriate in the case of projects creating completely distributed blockchain, such as Ethereum and Bitcoin. However, because creating such a project is not easy, many projects have created new virtual currencies to use for their Dapp or applications and services built by using smart contracts. Some tokens, such as the BNB token, guarantee returns by offering token buybacks.

As regulatory agencies have tightened control of token sales in many countries, more and more ICO projects no longer sell tokens to general investors, and, instead, offer only to qualified investors.

2.2 From ICO to STO

As the size of ICOs became larger, people in the financial industry became more and more involved in the virtual currency industry. Having noticed the contradiction of ICOs and securities regulations, they started raising funds by offering tokens that completely conform to securities regulations, known as security token offerings (STOs) . In September 2018, Elevated Returns, a shareholder of Regis Aspen Resort, securitized its real estate investment trust shares of St. Regis Aspen Resort by creating what is called the Aspen Coin and raised 18 million dollars by selling to eligible investors. The Aspen Coin is written on Ethereum and can be stored in Ethereum wallet. However, unlike ETH and BTC, Aspen Coins cannot be freely transferred from one wallet to another.

To fundraise using STO, it is necessary to create a new type of smart contract on Ethereum to keep the token in line with securities regulations. Such smart contracts, for example, need to restrict token trade, to record the nationalities of token purchasers, and to incorporate a system that makes it possible to reissue a password (private key) in case the original password is lost. However, implementing these functions requires the program developer to create central control over a blockchain token. If that is done, the resulting system becomes similar to the current centralized client/server network model. This pulls blockchain away from its original philosophy of decentralization. Many pure blockchain experts object to such a shift.

Ex-CEO of the largest Chinese ICO platform in 2017, James Gong, has compared STOs with WinFax. WinFax is a faxing software developed for Windows 3.x in the 1990s. It sends Windows documents directly to either a fax machine or a PC that can receive fax. Although not widely known, WinFax was a very popular program. A peculiar thing is that it transforms digital data on PC into analog data and sends it through a phone line so the data can be received by a fax machine. From the viewpoint of modern Internet users, WinFax appears to have gone against the trend of the Internet and its technological progress to transform analog communications into digital communications. However, before society realized the revolutionary change that the Internet was about to bring to personal computing, WinFax was a useful technology as an interface between the coming digital world and the analog world that was still in use.

STO may be at a position similar to that at which WinFax was in the 1990s. In other words, STO is a device that tries to go against the strong current transforming the conventional centralized financial system into the coming decentralized system. As society becomes familiar with the decentralized financial system, STOs may become less and less popular just like WinFax, which became less popular as society became familiar with the Internet and email. WinFax has helped shift people from analog communications into digital communications. Similarly, STO may help people to get acquainted with the decentralized financial system, which is currently forming.

3 ICO and Securities Regulations

Various approaches can be considered for regulating ICOs and tokens. We focus on the features of ICOs and tokens as securities and study their regulations in that context.

3.1 Types of Tokens and Proper Regulations

ICO is a generic term for issuing electronic tokens (or simply tokens) to raise funds from the public for entrepreneurial purposes. There are various types of tokens. In addition to the IOU tokens discussed in the previous section, virtual currencies that are issued on blockchain in exchange for IOU tokens are also referred to as tokens.

Different countries adopt different classifications for tokens in light of their economic functions and purposes. Below, we explain the Swiss classification, which is relatively simple and easy to understand. In February 2018, the Swiss Financial Market Supervisory Authority (FINMA) issued a guideline that classifies tokens into three categories by focusing on their economic function and purpose. They are:

1. **Payment token**: A payment token is a synonym for a virtual currency. It is used as a means of payment for goods and services and has nothing to do with other development projects.
2. **Utility token**: A utility token is a type of ticket that is to be used for acquiring a specific digital application or service.
3. **Asset token**: An asset token is the representation of a claim concerning assets, for example, to receive dividends and interest payments from companies and income-generating businesses.

Of course, there are many real-world tokens that do not fit one of these categories. FINMA points out that some tokens have features that overlap more than one of these categories.

The security token described in the previous section is included in the asset token under the FINMA classification. An asset token is similar to stocks and corporate bonds. It gives the token holder the right to receive dividends and property distribution from the business. For this reason, FINMA specifies that asset tokens are regulated as securities. In many countries, similar asset tokens are regulated as securities. In Japan as well, under the Financial Instruments and Exchange Act, an asset token is classified as a security as a group investment scheme share (Financial Instruments and Exchange Act Article 2, paragraph 2, item 5) and is considered to be subject to that regulation.

Payment tokens are currencies, and FINMA does not treat them as securities. Bitcoin is a good example of a payment token. It is also common in many countries that tokens that do not have features other than a currency are not treated as securities.

It has been argued that utility tokens as well are not like securities because they are just like tickets for using services. FINMA also states that if the sole purpose of a token is to give the right to use digital applications, the token is not regarded as a security but as a right to use services, so long as it does not function as an investment.

In this regard, the SEC has taken a position that whether a token is regarded as a security depends on its economic substance, not whether it is called a utility token (Munchee case. Dec. 11, 2017, Exclusion order dated). This case addressed whether the token that Munchee, which operates the restaurant evaluation app used on the iPhone, attempted to issue by ICO (named "MUN token") is a security. In its white paper, which explained the business of a company planning an ICO, Munchee emphasized that the value of the token issued by the ICO was expected to appreciate because of the following business plan. The company would issue MUN tokens to the users who uploaded pictures and reviews on restaurants that they visit, and, in the future, make it possible for MUN token holders to pay at the restaurants reviewed. Moreover, the company made firm commitment to make it possible for token holders to resell their tokens in multiple secondary markets. In light of these facts, the SEC concluded that although the MUN token did not promise to pay dividends, Munchee created a reasonable expectation among purchasers of MUN tokens that its value will appreciate once the company made the software application available to the public. In this finding, the SEC followed its conventional position that a device creating a reasonable expectation that investors will benefit from the business effort of the investee is an investment contract and is categorized as a security. This shows the SEC's position that tokens creating such an expectation are regarded as a security under US law. In short, although its issuer calls it a utility token, the MUN token, creating an expectation that its value will appreciate, is regarded as a security. This agrees with the FINMA guidelines.

On April 3, 2019, the SEC announced a framework to determine whether a particular digital asset falls in the category of an "investment contract" (Securities and Exchange Commission 2019a). The SEC clearly pointed out that the conventional test, described above in relation to Munchee, applies in determining whether the

ICOs and the sales of other digital assets are covered by the Securities Act. In addition, it provided various examples that may or may not be treated as an "investment contract." At the same time, the SEC communicated that the token that TurnKey Jet (TKJ) was about to issue is not regarded as an "investment contract" for the following reasons (Securities and Exchange Commission 2019b).

- TKJ will not use any funds from Token sales to develop the TKJ Platform, Network, or App, and each of these will be fully developed and operational at the time any Tokens are sold;
- the Tokens will be immediately usable for their intended functionality (purchasing air charter services) at the time they are sold;
- TKJ will restrict transfers of Tokens to TKJ Wallets only, and not to wallets external to the Platform;
- TKJ will sell Tokens at a price of 1 USD per Token throughout the life of the Program, and each Token will represent a TKJ obligation to supply air charter services at a value of 1 USD per Token;
- If TKJ offers to repurchase Tokens, it will only do so at a discount to the face value of the Tokens (1 USD per Token) that the holder seeks to resell to TKJ, unless a court within the United States orders TKJ to liquidate the Tokens; and
- The Token is marketed in a manner that emphasizes the functionality of the Token, and not the potential for any increase in the market value of the Token.

This shows that the SEC also takes into consideration technological innovation, while assuming that whether a token falls under the Securities Act is determined on a case-by-case basis regarding factual manners. Thus, it is apparent that the SEC is trying to establish clear criteria for blockchain token issuers.

3.2 Information Disclosure

If a token is regarded as a security under the laws of a particular country, before the issuance, the issuer is required to disclose material information concerning the issuer's business, although the requirements differ across countries. There are exceptions in which this requirement does not apply; for example, the cases in which targeted investors are limited to a small number of individuals or to professional informed investors. This requirement on information disclosure is to eliminate the so-called asymmetry of information; that is, to ensure that the investors who are interested in buying the security to have all the material information that would be relevant for the valuation of the issue. In short, the main purpose is to let investors make informed decisions.

The disclosure of information at the time of a security is referred to as initial disclosure. For the case in which the issuer's business continues after the initial issuance, periodic disclosure of information is required if the issuer's security is continuously circulated on the market over time. The holders of securities often purchase a security in hopes of recovering their investments by selling it later. For the secondary market of such securities to function properly, it is necessary for the sellers and buyers of the securities to evaluate the value of the securities based on the same information. Therefore, if issued securities are expected to be distributed, the issuers of the securities are required to periodically disclose important information on the securities. This is often referred to as continuous disclosure or ongoing disclosure.

If a token is identified as a security, the ICO for that token will usually be viewed as an act of soliciting purchases of securities to an unspecified and/or large number of people. The issuer is, therefore, required to disclose relevant information regarding the business relating to the token. Moreover, when the token is expected to be traded on the market over time, it should be assumed that the issuer will be required to disclose relevant information over time.

3.3 Blockchain Characteristics and Security Regulation Conformance

As discussed above, there are cases in which the ICOs on token are subject to securities regulations, and, therefore, to information disclosure requirements. However, as explained below, it is unclear whether applying securities regulations and requiring information disclosure is enough to protect the holders of tokens and those interested in investing in tokens.

First, there are many kinds of tokens, and their contents vary. In comparison with traditional securities such as stocks and bonds where the holder's right is legally established, it is unclear what kind of right you may obtain if you hold the token. That is why it is important to let investors know what right they will obtain and what they can do with the token. Therefore, it is undoubtedly important to require disclosure of information for token issuance. It is also possible to impose damages, criminal penalties, and administrative sanctions under securities laws on those who give false or misleading information. At this moment, there is no legal protection for a token holder's right to monitor the progress of the project, nor is the method of monitoring the progress stipulated. Under corporate law, stockholders are given the right to attend a general meeting of shareholders and make decisions on important matters and to receive business reports and financial statements. In contrast, the legal relationship between the token holders and the token issuer is unclear, for there is no legal provision for the nature of the token. As such, it is not clear what token holders can claim against the token issuer or what rights they have. At this moment, it is unclear whether any contractual relationship exists between the token holder and the token issuer, and what contents the contract, if it exists, may have. Therefore, for now, we can only take a case-by-case approach.

Second, blockchain technology is characterized by its ability to provide open-source and distributed ledgers. In a typical blockchain project, the protocol and software will be open to the public upon completion; once publicly released, the original developers cannot modify the contents freely. It is the nature of open-source programs that, once publicly released, there are no owners of the system/network and thus no administrator can be identified. The developer is not obligated to perform maintenance after completion. Even if the developer of the project funded by an ICO is asked to perform continuous disclosure, once the project becomes public, the developer will no longer be either the owner or the administrator. Under such circumstances, it is unclear whether such continuous disclosure is possible.

Some projects do not adopt an open-source model, in which case continuous disclosure is theoretically possible. However, because problems on protocol and software are most of the time not understandable for ordinary investors, the problems arising from asymmetric information might be even more serious.

Logically speaking, it is difficult to establish the relationship between the business performance to which a token is linked and the value of the token except for asset tokens for which the distribution of dividends and a residual claim are explicitly guaranteed. If, like the MUN token issue, the token issuer explicitly explains to investors that the token value is likely to go up once the project become publicly available, it is not very clear how the token value is affected by information on the development of the project and on business performance after the public release of the project. If no clear explanation is given as to why the token value will rise, the information disclosed could become misleading rather than informative, although the positive aspect of information disclosure should not be discounted.

Third, generally speaking, it is extremely difficult for nonexperts to evaluate the success probability of a new project. This implies that if information is completely disclosed before an ICO, it is unclear whether it is permissible to accept investment from anyone. This is not limited to token issuances; the exact same issue arises in the case of investment in venture companies. In that case, experts in venture investment such as venture capital companies examine and evaluate a business model in a direct interview with an entrepreneur; this process is called due diligence. Usually, at this stage, venture companies do not seek investment from the general public but rather invite a few specific experts. For this reason, venture capital offerings of stocks are treated as an exception to the SEC's disclosure requirements. Typically, venture capital investors negotiate out a deal with entrepreneurs with respect to various rights and obligations on equity investment.

An IPO of corporate shares to the public is conducted after a company's business is expected to generate profits without big risks. In a typical IPO, an investment bank or securities company underwrites the initially offered shares; that is, they purchase the entire offer at a price negotiated right before the IPO. In the real world, some IPOs fail, meaning that the initial market price of a share is set below the negotiated price. To avoid such failures, even IPOs are subject to a process in which the investment bank or securities company fully evaluate the business of an equity issuer before the IPO.

In short, before corporate shares are made available to the general public for investment, there is a long process of evaluating companies at the stages of venture capital investment and IPO underwriting.

It could be argued that an ICO requires even deeper scrutiny of a project than an IPO, because ordinary investors are, at least at this moment, far less familiar with the technological aspects of an ICO than general businesses that are represented by an IPO. Even if disclosure of information is sufficient for an expert's evaluation, it may not be appropriate to solicit investment from those who are not experts at the stage at which the business plan of a project is subject to a large risk.

Fourth, there is an important question as to which country's security regulations should govern an ICO. In many ICOs, investments have been made in virtual currency through the Internet; for example, MUN tokens were available to individuals not only in the USA but also in every other country. In that case, an important question is: under the regulations of which country are investors protected? In all countries, securities laws are drafted primarily to protect domestic investors. Moreover, the details of securities laws and regulations differ across countries. As a result, the regulation of ICOs involves rather messy international legal issues.

3.4 Desirable ICOs

If the future value of a token may depend on the success or failure of a particular project, it may not be appropriate to allow an issuer to solicit investment from ordinary investors before the issuer completes the project. This is also the case even if the token issuer explains that the project is not yet developed.

In practice, this concern could be substantially eliminated by treating the token as a security. If a token is recognized as a security, and if the ICO is subject to both initial and continuous disclosure of information under the securities law, it will be a considerable burden on the token issuer. As a result, token issuers will avoid an ICO, which subjects the issuer to the disclosure restrictions. Specifically, as in the case of stocks, the company will offer tokens only to certain specialists such as venture capital and prohibit the transfer of tokens by investors who have obtained tokens for the time being. A token ICO will be conducted when the development of the project has progressed considerably. At that time, issuance disclosure and subsequent disclosure will also be required if securities regulations are applied.

Even if a project is to develop an application that is absolutely distributed and decentralized, and if the developer does not have any right after the development is completed, it may have a feature of a utility token that is associated with the right to use some service offered by the software. Even in that case, if the value of the token is affected by the state of that service, continuous disclosure should be required with respect to the service, once the token starts circulating on the open market. In such continuous disclosure, care must be taken that the disclosed information does not mislead investors with respect to the relationship between the success or failure of the business and the value of the token.

For payment tokens, their values are not related to the success or failure of other projects. In that case, a token may be a security. For tokens that are not subject to securities regulations, it is not expected that ICOs will be suddenly barred. Even in that case, certain types of information should be disclosed. They are: (1) the identity and history the token issuer (and the director of the issuer if the issuer is a corporation); (2) the current status, development schedule, and technical issues of the program/protocol; (3) the rights guaranteed by the program/protocol upon completion; (4) plans for future maintenance and the way to cover the resulting costs; and (5) methods for program/protocol modification in the future. Moreover, it is important to disclose details on the protocol and the system of protocol maintenance in the future; more specifically, for the case in which a foundation organized by experts is expected to conduct voluntary evaluations and maintenance, the process of organizing the foundation should be explained. In addition, it may be worth considering having third-party experts evaluate the program or protocol and to disclose the evaluation.

Of course, it is of utmost importance to explain the content of the token and the right that comes with ownership of the token. This implies that regardless of the type of token (i.e., whether it falls into the category of a security), it is necessary to disclose accurate information on the ICO, including: (1) the function/use of the token; (2) legal rights of token holders and legal obligations of the token issuer; (3) method of issuance (as well as future issues); (4) volume of tokens owned by the token issuer; (5) objective explanation and analysis on token value; (6) future circulation of the tokens; (7) use of funds; and (8) information on risk factors. Needless to say, it is important to make proper information disclosure so as to avoid speculative activities.

4 Towards Building a Healthy Blockchain Ecosystem

Because blockchain technology is introduced with Bitcoin, many countries are considering adopting financial regulations for the blockchain industry. Japan is no exception.

Every new business is associated with new risks. When Edison started a power company, people suffered from power failures and fires caused by electrical leakage; some people were electrocuted in avoidable careless accidents.

The aim of this book is not just to explain virtual currencies but to study blockchain technology, which by creating distributed ledgers makes it possible to safely and efficiently use personal and industrial data in production processes. Examples might include a small farmer's plant-by-plant agricultural data, health data relating to lifestyle-related diseases, and congestion data on city traffic. Blockchain technology will make it possible to utilize these types of data without intruding personal privacy and trade secrets. If such data were to become available, the amount of agricultural waste products may be reduced, middle-aged and older people could use data to modify lifestyle habits to gain health benefits, and forecasts of traffic congestion may become readily available for drivers. Furthermore, blockchain technology will open the possibility that various digital assets and utility tokens will be made available by DApps. Moreover, this technology may create a stable virtual currency that makes various micropayments possible.

Placed in this broad perspective, issues surrounding blockchain technology boil down to the choice of an ecosystem in which human life faces digital data as productive resources. Next, we consider the financing of the startup phase and the credibility of a virtual currency.

4.1 Professional Market for Financing

In the United States, on the one hand, ICO regulations are built on the Securities Act. In Japan, on the other hand, they are studied in the context of the Financial Instruments and Exchange Act. Because there is no proof of success for a business startup, the informational asymmetry between an entrepreneur and ordinary investors must be heeded. It is important to build an ecosystem in which blockchain projects are funded by professional investors, who go through careful due diligence.

An ICO is based on a business model that issues tokens to raise funds by taking advantage of the features of blockchain technology. However, just like usual startups, it is possible to raise funds from investment professionals. In light of the original philosophy of blockchain technology, at the same time, the success of a blockchain project may not depend on that of an ICO.

Silicon Valley has produced many successful Internet companies such as Hewlett Packard, Apple, and Google. In that region, there is a global concentration of venture capitalists, who actively invest in new businesses. One of the areas in which those investors have competed against each other is FinTech, which is the new applications, processes, products, or business models in the financial services industry, providing various financial services through the Internet.

In the field of FinTech, many startups competed in the early 2010s with a focus in the USA, the United Kingdom, and Ireland. After several years, however, only a very small number of projects survived. A number of venture capitalists have participated as investors in this process. However, in the end, only a handful of Silicon Valley investors specializing in FinTech have become successful. These investors, in addition to having financial knowledge, were familiar with the state of the art at the forefront of algorithm development.

It is foreseeable that the blockchain industry will follow a similar course. Investors should not only have a strong insight into a business model but also should be familiar with algorithm development in many of the areas discussed in this book. Blockchain technology has features that are unique relative to conventional targets for investment. Multiple individuals cooperate to develop algorithms and make their contents publicly available, which is often called the open-source model. The operating entity of a business that uses the algorithm may be an entity that is not even a joint-stock company. If it is not a legal entity, a completely new device is necessary to distribute the return from investments to investors. From such an ambiguity, an innovation may emerge that is suitable for projects based on blockchain technology.

4.2 Reliability of Payment Tokens

An important issue is how to keep payment tokens credible. Whether virtual currency possesses the three functions of money (the unit of value, the medium of exchange, and the store of value) depends on whether the algorithm possesses these three functions. Experiences has accumulated at monetary authorities and central banks with respect to the stabilization of the value of the existing currency system. Blockchain technology has shown that this role of monetary authorities and central banks may be substituted with an algorithm. Countries adopt different monetary policies; as a result, degrees of freedom that countries' central banks have differ across countries. The virtual currency is not subject to such restrictions. It is quite possible that a virtual currency based on blockchain technology would offer the ecosystem a more reliable currency system than the current monetary systems.

However, macro economies are constantly fluctuating and are subject to big shocks. The central bank, as the keeper of the currency, can manage such crises. It is well known that in an unprecedented situation such as the Lehman shock, stock market players in each country continue to trade by following a preset algorithm, which enlarged the existing crisis.

Over the past 10 years, Bitcoin has successfully shown its basic reliability as a currency. However, its value has fluctuated significantly. This is expected from the systematic design of Bitcoin's algorithm. Thus, a question arises as to what kind of algorithm may function better as a currency. It is an important joint task for economists and computer scientists to come up with the basis of an algorithm-based currency that people can fully trust.

4.3 Application Safety and Quality

Blockchain technology has the advantage of being able to process data in a distributed manner without giving the data to a particular group of people. If a mechanism can be created that eliminates government regulations imposing responsibility for the safety and quality of applications on specific people, blockchain technology can be put to the most efficient use. This is reflected in the opinion that STO should be transitional, which is feared to harm the healthy development of distributed algorithms.

If the application is open source, it must be assumed that the person who created the application is not responsible for managing the resulting business. How then does one ensure the safety and quality of the application?

If an application is open source, it is desirable to have a third party that always checks the safety and quality of the application, to announce potential risks, and to acknowledge that a proper fix is made. An audit corporation may provide such a service in the way that bond credit rating companies do. However, because technological progress is very fast, a peer-review system for applications may be more suitable.

In particular, the certification of personal data protection and trade secret retention can be thought of as the basis for the sound development of the blockchain industry. Even if no problem is noticed at the time of application development, it is likely to become necessary to deal with new issues on computer security, because unforeseen issues can always occur. The peer-review system may be effective for dealing with these problems.

One of the infrastructures that fostered Japanese industrialization after World War II is the Japan Industrial Standard System, which is known as the JIS mark. Although this system involved both compulsory and voluntary standards, from a certain time, a bold shift to voluntary standards was initiated so as to leave the private sector's own initiatives to evaluate the safety and quality of a product. This is because the peer-review system using private experts was, and has been, regarded as reliable and as better in promoting innovation.

If applications have a large number of users, it may be a good idea to create more than one peer-review system for quality examination. If those peer-review systems compete with each other, the quality of reviews will naturally rise, which should make it possible to evaluate applications with a high standard based on the newest technological development and the highest expertise.

It is desirable that the developers of blockchain businesses create collaboratively multiple peer-review systems and protect the safety and quality of their applications. In that way, innovation can be made active without harming the merits and potential of the distributed ledger technology.

4.4 *Creation of an International Ecosystem Beyond Borders*

Although civil contracts are based on the principle of freedom of contract, they must conform to various laws and regulations for the purpose of security of transactions, securing equality of parties, and safety and security of society. Blockchain technology has great advantages in freely exchanging data across borders. Given the nature of trading personal and corporate data, it is necessary to verify in advance each country's laws and regulations from various points of view, not only for investment contracts but also for user terms and conditions. In addition, in the case of an application created by open source, it must be assumed that the operating entity cannot be identified; as a result, a problem arises as to who is responsible for contracts and terms.

With regard to contracts and terms that provide services, as represented by smart contracts, there may be a need for a system that allows legal and regulatory experts in each country to examine the contents and to determine that there are no problems. While each country has one or more actors, it will also be necessary to have an international Internet network that provides information on the compatibility of each country's legal system. On the one hand, it may be a good idea to create a non-governmental international organization similar to the International Organization for Standardization (ISO) for international dispute resolution. On the other hand, some may desire governmental involvement in such a process. We believe that the international community is at the stage where it can start a discussion on this issue.

Cases:

"Chandelor v. Lopus," 79 Eng. Rep. 3 (1603).
"United Housing Foundation, Inc. v. Foreman," 421 U.S. 837 (1975).
"Securities and Exchange Commission v. W. J. Howey Co.," 328 U.S. 293 (1946).

References

Gonson P (2003) Letter to the Securities and Exchange Commission, July 10, 2003

Lowenthal J (1891) Caveat Emptor, Cornell Law School, downloaded at Cornell Law Library, Scholarship@Cornell Law: A Digital Repository

Pu S, Yano M (2020) Market quality approach to IoT Data on blockchain big data. In: Yano M et al (eds) Blockchain and crypto currency: a high-quality marketplace for crypto data. Springer

Securities and Exchange Commission (2003) No Action, Interpretive and/or Exemptive Letter: The Ticket Reserve, Inc., September 11, 2003

Securities and Exchange Commission (2019a). Framework for "investment contract" analysis of digital assets, modified, April 3, 2019

Securities and Exchange Commission (2019b) Response of the division of corporation finance. RE: TurnKey Jet, Inc., Incoming letter dated April 2, 2019. April 3, 2019

Seligman J (1982) The transformation of wall street. Houghton Mifflin, Boston

Yano M (2019) Market quality theory and the Coase theorem in the presence of transaction costs, RIETI DP19-E-097

Makoto Yano is Chairman of the Research Institute of Economy, Trade and Industry (RIETI); he is also a specially appointed professor at Kyoto University, Jochi University, and Chubu University. He is an internationally known researcher who has made a number of substantial contributions in international trade, market theory, and especially on economic dynamics. His contributions in economic dynamics, for example, are represented by articles in *Econometrica* in 1995 and the *Journal of Economic Theory* in 1996, which explained the conditions under which general economic equilibrium shows chaotic behavior. His 1998 *Econometrica* article is recognized as the latest most important work on the characterization of dynamic general equilibrium.

Besides those rather theoretical works, Prof. Yano has also provided influential insights on contemporary real-world phenomena. Those include transfer problems (*American Economic Review*, 1999), voluntary export restraints (*International Economic Review* [IER], 1995), and trade conflicts (IER, 1998), on which there have been a number of follow-up papers.

His recent research on "market quality" addresses various problems in modern economies, including the financial market crisis since 2008 and the recent nuclear accidents in Japan, from the point of view of market quality—a new economic concept that Prof. Yano has developed and is applying to Japanese and international markets. Concerning quality of competition, quality of information, and quality of products, market quality is defined as an index jointly determined by the efficiency of an allocation and the fairness of the prices that are achieved in a market. Prof. Yano received a B.A. in economics from The University of Tokyo in 1971 and a Ph.D. in economics from The University of Rochester in 1981.

Chris Dai is the CEO and co-founder of Leland Capital, Recika Co., Ltd., and CEO of LongHash Japan. He has a broad range of business management and investment experience. He was formerly the COO/CIO of Yixing SCM (an international logistics provider), a consultant at Accenture, and a co-founder of multiple ventures. Starting in 2013, Mr. Dai was one of the early investors in Bitcoin and Ethereum. To promote the understanding of blockchain's true value, he joined the Research Institute of Economy, Trade and Industry's blockchain research team. He received a B.S. in management science and engineering from Stanford University in 2004.

Kenichi Masuda has been a partner at the law firm of Anderson, Mori & Tomotsune since 1997. He graduated from The University of Tokyo in 1986. After completing work at the Judicial Research and Training Institute, he was admitted to the bar in Japan and joined the law firm in 1988. He graduated from The University of Chicago Law School in 1992 and was admitted to the bar of the State of New York in 1993.

Mr. Masuda has extensive experience in advising foreign clients and is familiar with cross-border issues, in particular, mergers and acquisitions of listed and unlisted businesses, joint ventures, and other cross-border investments, as well as corporate restructuring. The scope of his experience also includes assisting and representing venture companies and establishing venture capital or other private equity funds. He regularly provides legal services on employment and labor union relations (including representation of client companies in court and other dispute-resolution forums), real property transactions, intellectual property issues, and general corporate and commercial matters.

Mr. Masuda currently teaches at The University of Tokyo Law School as a visiting professor.

Yoshio Kishimoto is director general of International Policy for Small and Medium-Sized Enterprises (SMEs), Ministry of Economy, International Trade and Industry. He was vice president of the Research Institute of Economy, International Trade and Industry with Professor Yano.

He has held various positions in METI including head of the Environment and Economy Office, Business Support Division of the SME Agency, and director general of the Kyushu Bureau of METI. He received his M.A. in international affairs from Columbia University in 1992 and a Bachelor of Law degree from The University of Tokyo in 1985.

Chapter 8
Bitcoin and Blockchain Technology

Kazumasa Omote and Makoto Yano

A ledger can be defined as a "book of permanent record." With modern information technology, data have become economic resources if they are associated with exclusive owners and put into a ledger. It is shown in Chaps. 3 and 4 that IoT data can be transformed into productive resources while Chaps. 5 and 6 show that transaction data can be turned into money-like bank deposit currencies.

Blockchain is a technology that put data into such a ledger without a central authority like banks managing deposit currencies. Instead, many independent people with technical knowledge contribute to put together a ledger that associates data pieces with their owners. In this chapter, we explain this technology by focusing on the original blockchain for Bitcoin.

The Bitcoin blockchain is the first decentralized ledger that turned data into an economic resource. Such a ledger must have several basic features:

1. Timestamps
2. Immutability
3. Accuracy
4. Uniqueness
5. Authenticity

This article is based on our final report to the study group "Blockchain and Society 5.0—The Creation of a New Marketplace based on Distributed Consensus" at the Research Institute of Economy, Trade, and Industry (RIETI) . We are grateful to all the participants for useful discussions and, in particular, to Chris Dai for insightful comments. The second author gratefully acknowledges the financial support of a Grant-in-Aid for Scientific Research (A) (#16H02015) from the Japan Society for the Promotion of Science.

K. Omote
University of Tsukuba, Tsukuba, Japan

M. Yano (✉)
Research Institute of Economy, Trade and Industry (RIETI), Tokyo, Japan
e-mail: yano-makoto@rieti.go.jp

M. Yano et al. (eds.), *Blockchain and Crypto Currency*,
Economics, Law, and Institutions in Asia Pacific,
https://doi.org/10.1007/978-981-15-3376-1_8

A timestamp is a marker that specifies the time and date at which a record is made. Putting a timestamp on each piece of data is important if the ownership of a data piece changes overtime. For example, if a ledger is for recording the ownership of properties, it would become impossible to tell who owns a particular property at a particular moment without a timestamp.

By immutability, we mean that data cannot be tampered with or altered by malicious attack. This implies that no one can make a counterfeit version of an existing ledger.

Accuracy implies that a ledger must record data correctly and satisfy any constraints imposed on the ledger. For example, a ledger for monetary transactions must ensure that for each transaction, no one can spend more than the existing balance in his/her account.

Uniqueness implies that every ledger must be a unique book of record for that particular kind. If two different books of record are created, it will invite disputes; for example, if a ledger is to record the ownership of land, each piece of land must be associated with a unique owner. Historically, many territorial disputes have resulted from the failure to maintain a unique book of record of land ownership.

By authenticity, we mean that each data piece on the ledger must describe the exact intention of its owner. If it is a ledger for monetary transactions that a bank maintains, records on deposits to or withdrawals from accounts must be conducted in the exact way in which owners intend. If a transaction is to be made through an automatic teller machine (ATM), this could be achieved by using the proper password for the account, which assures that an order is authentic.

Conventional ledgers have been maintained by central authorities; records on bank transactions by banks and those on marital status by local governments, and so on. Blockchain technology makes it possible to build such a ledger in a decentralized manner without any central authority. Instead, a blockchain is based on algorithms that computers can follow.

It is not an easy task to come up with such algorithms. In what follows, we explain the implementation of such an algorithm by focusing on the Bitcoin blockchain, which was the first to show the potential of a decentralized algorithm-based ledger system.

The Bitcoin algorithm adopts four important ideas in designing a monetary ledger. They are:

1. Chain of blocks
2. Proof-of-work
3. Decentralized consensus algorithm
4. Open-key cryptographic accounts

1 Chain of Blocks

In a blockchain, a block is a file containing data with a timestamp. Bitcoin blockchain is a chain that connects blocks in one single row. Every time a new block is built, this is attached to the most recent block on the chain.

2 Proof-of-Work

To build a ledger, a new block must be "glued" to the most recent block. A cryptographic riddle plays the role of glue that permanently connects a block to the previous block. It takes a large amount of computing power (i.e., electricity) to solve this riddle. This process is referred to as proof-of-work, implying that a block embedded into a blockchain shows that a sufficient amount of computing power was expended for its creation.

Once a block is built, it is converted into a cryptographic riddle. To understand this riddle, it is necessary to know a cryptographic algorithm called a secure hash algorithm (SHA). The SHA transforms any digital data of any length into a unique sequence of seemingly random numerals with a fixed length. A number of SHAs have been developed. The most common algorithm currently is called SHA 256, which transforms any sentence into a 256-digit number in the binary numeral system. For example, SHA 256 transforms the word "blockchain" into

SHA (blockchain)
=EF7797E13D3A75526946A3BCF00DAEC9
FC9C9C4D51DDC7CC5DF888F74DD434D1 (1)

which is expressed in the hexadecimal numeral system (with numerals 0–9 and letters A–F). This value is called the hash value of word "blockchain" by SHA 256.

SHAs are designed in such a way that it is practically impossible to guess the original sentence from a hash value. A particular sentence is always translated into the same hash value. Moreover, the chance with which two different sentences are associated with an identical hash value is practically zero.

One use of a SHA is to store a password. For example, a password for an ATM must be stored in association with an account number. If passwords were stored in the naked values chosen by account owners, it would create a huge problem if passwords were stolen. A secure hash algorithm is useful to hide a password from anyone other than the associated account owner. Even if someone sees the hash value of the password associated with an account, he/she can never find the password. At the same time, whether the password inputted into an ATM is authentic can be easily determined by transforming the inputted password by the SHA adopted by the bank.

The cryptographic riddle called proof-of-work requires a sequence of numerals that can be attached to the end of a particular sentence so that the hash value of the particular sentence plus the attached sequence starts with X number of zeros that is required by the algorithm. If the proof-of-work riddle asks to find a sequence of numerals to attach to "blockchain" so that the first number of the hash value is zero, a solution is the sequence of 34 zeros at the end of the word "blockchain." That is to say,

SHA(blockchain0000000000000000000000000000000000)
= 088C389A0BC33DE6A7D8DD9012DBD6
C5E9276B94C2639E72725F40E98A7163AA (2)

If a 16-digit hash value is a sequence of randomly selected numerals from 1 through F (actually it is not), the probability with which the first number is zero is 1/16, and that for the first two numbers is $1/16^2$. Thus, it is clear that there are many solutions for each proof-of-work riddle. Moreover, as the required number of zeros is increased, it becomes increasingly difficult to find a solution where a sequence of numerals is attached to a given sentence so that zeros will line up at the beginning of the value as the algorithm requires.

If this algorithm is used for filing a piece of information (or if "blockchain" is the piece to be filed) , it can serve as a simple proof that a certain computing time is spent before filing the information. This is because it takes time to find a correct sequence of numerals to attach to a message, and it is very easy to check whether the attached sequence is correct. For this reason, the algorithm is regarded as providing a proof-of-work.

A proof-of-work algorithm was invented in 1997 for software called Hashcash. This software separates meaningful emails from spam mails. For example, if every nonspam mail is required to include a solution that lines up a certain number of zeros at the beginning of the hash value of email sentences, it takes a certain length of computing time before a sender sends out the email. Because of the costly computing time, no spam sender dares to solve the riddle imposed by Hashcash, and no spam mails are delivered with the solution to the riddle. As a result, mail receivers can separate real mails (with solutions to the riddle) from spam mails.

The Bitcoin blockchain adopts a proof-of-work algorithm. To create and attach a new block to the existing chain, it is required to find a solution such that a specific number of zeros lines up at the beginning of the hash value of the solution added to what is written in the existing block and to write the solution in the new block. The number of zeros that the Bitcoin blockchain requires is set in such a way that it takes, on average, about 10 min for a fast computer to find a solution.

This wipes out any incentive to tamper with a blockchain because rewriting part or all of blocks on a chain requires solving the riddles all over again, which is extremely costly. In short, a blockchain built on a proof-of-work algorithm is immutable.

3 Decentralized Consensus Algorithm

Blockchain technology makes it possible to build an accurate ledger by relying not on a central authority but on an algorithm involving many independent people or computers called network nodes. This algorithm is called a (decentralized) consensus algorithm.

To create a ledger in a decentralized manner, it is important to provide incentives for people to willingly contribute to building a ledger. In the Bitcoin blockchain, this incentive is created by separating people who make use of a ledger (users), recording transfers of money between user accounts, from those who add new records to the ledger. An individual who wants to record a transfer of money posts a transaction with a proposed transaction fee. Because the maximum size of each block is fixed, a recorder can select only a few from the pool of transactions and put together a new block. For a particular recorder to place his/her block to the existing blockchain, as discussed above, he/she must be the first to solve the cryptographic riddle created from the latest block of the chain. To attract a sufficiently large number of recorders, a fixed amount of money is given as a prize to any recorder who actually adds a new block to the chain. If this prize is sufficiently large, many people will participate in creating new blocks. No matter how many recorders participating in the creation of a new block at a particular point of time, only one recorder can get the prize. This process is similar to looking for gold in a gold mine and therefore is referred to as "mining." People who run mining operations and maintain computers that record new blocks are called "miners".

Another way of looking at this process is to think of the group of miners as a computer network connected through the Internet. Miners are network nodes. The entire blockchain is stored on each node. Each node operates independently according to the node's own will.

The primary requirement for a ledger is accuracy. Although a proof-of-work algorithm prevents a ledger from being spammed, it is not enough to maintain the accuracy of a ledger. If a block contains false information, it must not be added to a blockchain. For a conventional ledger like a deposit currency, there is a central authority that single-handedly maintains accuracy.

The Bitcoin blockchain adopts a decentralized consensus algorithm. When a particular node joins the network, it is randomly associated with several existing nodes. Once a particular node puts a new block together and solves the riddle, it announces the new block to the associated nodes. Those associated nodes independently check if the new block contains any errors. If they find no error, they announce the new block to the entire network.[1] If the associated nodes find errors, they ignore the block, in which case no other nodes will know the new block. Through this process, the accuracy of blocks can be maintained.

Another important requirement for a ledger is its uniqueness; if it were possible that multiple books of records were created, they could not serve as a ledger. The Bitcoin blockchain is, however, subject to the possibility that multiple chains are

[1] If you operate a full node, there is a strong incentive to make such an announcement immediately. If you run a full node that is not broadcasting transactions, then when a transaction is made, it becomes immediately obvious to peers as to where that transaction originated. The incentive is to preserve your privacy. Even with a delayed broadcast, you would still be risking privacy because peers would likely become aware of the transaction first from other peers; then as soon as they see you broadcast a transaction that they had not seen from elsewhere, it would be reasonable for them to assume the transaction came from you.

built. As a result, there is a good chance that more than one node will solve the current riddle.

If more than one node succeeds, a blockchain bifurcates; the chain on some nodes will become different from that on other nodes after the point of bifurcation. To correct such a situation and to maintain a single chain, the Bitcoin algorithm sets a rule that the longest existing chain be perceived as the valid chain. If a chain bifurcates into two, at the point of bifurcation, the two chains have the same length, most likely, with different blocks at the end presenting different riddles. Because the length of time that is needed to solve a riddle is completely random, the length of one chain will quickly become longer than the other. As soon as this occurs, most nodes will start working on solving the riddle presented by the longer chain, and the shorter chain will quickly be ignored.

This implies that even if a block is created by solving a proof-of-work riddle, it does not imply that the block (and transactions in the block) will be recorded permanently. That is, those transactions could be recorded in a chain that will later become shorter than another, and, as a result, be forgotten.

4 Open-Key Cryptographic Accounts

Another important issue in building a ledger for the activities of individuals is to make sure that recording is prompted by the wills of the individuals conducting the activities. If a ledger is to record transfers of money from one account to another, the recording must reflect exactly what account owners want. However, how can miners tell that an application for recording a monetary transfer from an account is actually made by the owner of the account? In the case of a bank transfer, it is easy; the bank can simply check if the person asking for a transfer knows the password of the account. However, this task is not as simple if the record is to be produced in a decentralized manner.

Blockchain technology overcomes this difficulty by using "public-key cryptography," which gives a pair of keys to encrypt and decrypt a text. If a text is encrypted by one of the two keys, the resulting encrypted text can be decrypted into the original text by the other key. It is designed in such a way that it is impossible to identify one key from the other key.

Of course, it is possible for two parties to use a public-key cryptography to communicate just between themselves by assigning one of the two keys to one party and the other key to the other party. However, more common usage is to make one of the two keys public, which explains the terminology of public-key cryptography.

One use of public-key cryptography is to receive a message confidentially. For that purpose, a message receiver can create a pair of keys, make one of the keys public and keeping the other key private. If a sender of a message encrypts a message with the public key and sends it to the receiver, the receiver can receive the message by decrypting it with the private key.

Another use is for attaching a digital signature to prove that a message is from the sender and not from another individual. For this purpose, a sender can encrypt a message with a private key and send both the encrypted message by the paired public key and the original message. By using the received public key, the receiver can decrypt the encrypted message. If the resulting decrypted message is the same as the original message, which is sent separately, the receiver can be sure that the sender of the message is the person who knows the private key that is paired with the public key.

This method of digital signature is used by the Bitcoin blockchain. In creating a new account for Bitcoin, a random number is chosen first. By using a public-key cipher, this random number is transformed into the private key. This private key is then transformed into the paired public key. A Bitcoin account is produced from the public key. The public key is announced throughout the Internet. In essence, the public key serves as the base for a user's account whereas the private key serves as the password for the account. The account owner encrypts transactions with the private key and sends both the encrypted transaction and the original transaction, from which the miners can confirm authenticity of the transaction.

5 Concluding Remarks

The Bitcoin blockchain was the first to demonstrate that a ledger, an immutable, accurate, and unique book of record, can be built on the Internet in a decentralized manner. While this process has been accepted with great enthusiasm by many, a number of weak points have also been exposed. Currently, Bitcoin and other virtual currencies function as speculative instruments rather than as mediums of exchange. They are often used for trading illegal commodities such as drugs and for money laundering. These problems may be dealt with as society becomes better informed of what blockchains can do and what they cannot do.

A more fundamental problem may be that proof-of-work blockchains require a large amount of electricity for solving crypto riddles; an extremely large number of miners use their computers to solve blockchain riddles. However, as discussed in Chap. 5, what is attractive about virtual currencies is that production is not costly, which makes it possible to equate the marginal cost of money to the marginal utility of money. This is a necessary condition for efficient use of private goods; traditionally, money has been put outside of this efficiency consideration because goods with no value (like paper) has been used as money.

The Bitcoin blockchain is important because it has demonstrated that a deposit currency can be created fairly inexpensively in a decentralized manner. Once the possibility of such a technology is realized, many other new technologies will be developed that can offer much more than just money at a much cheaper cost.

Kazumasa Omote received his Ph.D. degree in information science from the Japan Advanced Institute of Science and Technology (JAIST) in 2002. He worked at Fujitsu Laboratories, Ltd., from 2002 to 2008 and was engaged in research and development for network security. He was a research assistant professor at JAIST from 2008 and an associate professor there from 2011. He has been an associate professor at the University of Tsukuba since 2016. His research interests include applied cryptography and network security. He is a member of the Institute of Electronics, Information and Communication Engineers (IEICE) and the Information Processing Society of Japan (IPSJ).

Makoto Yano is Chairman of the Research Institute of Economy, Trade and Industry (RIETI); he is also a specially appointed professor at Kyoto University, Jochi University, and Chubu University. He is an internationally known researcher who has made a number of substantial contributions in international trade, market theory, and especially on economic dynamics. His contributions in economic dynamics, for example, are represented by articles in *Econometrica* in 1995 and the *Journal of Economic Theory* in 1996, which explained the conditions under which general economic equilibrium shows chaotic behavior. His 1998 *Econometrica* article is recognized as the latest most important work on the characterization of dynamic general equilibrium.

Besides those rather theoretical works, Prof. Yano has also provided influential insights on contemporary real-world phenomena. Those include transfer problems (*American Economic Review*, 1999), voluntary export restraints (*International Economic Review* [IER], 1995), and trade conflicts (IER, 1998), on which there have been a number of follow-up papers.

His recent research on "market quality" addresses various problems in modern economies, including the financial market crisis since 2008 and the recent nuclear accidents in Japan, from the point of view of market quality—a new economic concept that Prof. Yano has developed and is applying to Japanese and international markets. Concerning quality of competition, quality of information, and quality of products, market quality is defined as an index jointly determined by the efficiency of an allocation and the fairness of the prices that are achieved in a market.

Prof. Yano received a B.A. in economics from The University of Tokyo in 1971 and a Ph.D. in economics from The University of Rochester in 1981.

Correction to: Blockchain and Crypto Currency

Makoto Yano, Chris Dai, Kenichi Masuda and Yoshio Kishimoto

Correction to: M. Yano et al. (eds.), *Blockchain and Crypto Currency*, Economics, Law, and Institutions in Asia Pacific, https://doi.org/10.1007/978-981-15-3376-1

The original version of the book was inadvertently published with incorrect book title and coeditors' affiliations in the front matter. The corrected book has been updated with the changes.

The updated version of the book can be found at
https://doi.org/10.1007/978-981-15-3376-1

M. Yano et al. (eds.), *Blockchain and Crypto Currency*,
Economics, Law, and Institutions in Asia Pacific,
https://doi.org/10.1007/978-981-15-3376-1_9

Index

M. Yano et al. (eds.), *Blockchain and Crypto Currency*, Economics, Law, and Institutions in Asia Pacific,
https://doi.org/10.1007/978-981-15-3376-1

The manufacturer's authorised representative in the EU is Springer Nature Customer Service Centre GmbH, Europaplatz 3, 69115 Heidelberg, Germany. If you have any concerns regarding our products, please contact ProductSafety@springernature.com

Printed and bound by CPI Group (UK) Ltd, Croydon, CR0 4YY
05/10/2026
02228153-0004